204 Fold & Say® Social Skills

by Deena E. Mahler, M.S., CCC-SLP
Edited by Molly Y. DeShong, Thomas Webber & Amy Jundi
Illustrated by Steve Barr, Jack Vaughan, and Ryan Bradburn

Copyright ©2002, SUPER DUPER® PUBLICATIONS, a division of Super Duper®, Inc. All rights reserved. Permission is granted for the user to reproduce the material contained herein in limited form for classroom use only. Reproduction of this material for an entire school or school system is strictly prohibited. No part of this material may be reproduced (except as noted above), stored in a retrieval system, or transmitted in any form or by any means (mechanically, electronically, recording, web, etc.) without the prior written consent and approval of Super Duper® Publications.

www.superduperinc.com
1-800-277-8737

#BK-293
ISBN 978-1-58650-208-9

Dedication

This book is dedicated to all of the children
I have had the privilege of educating.
You inspire me.

Deena E. Mahler, M.S., CCC-SLP

Introduction

Fold & Say® Social Skills is a collection of little books which present everyday social situations found at school, at home, and in the community. Each "mini-story" challenges students to develop their social skills in two ways. First, students look at/read about a common social situation, and decide "what happens next." Students tell about, write about, or draw a picture of this "next" event. Second, students answer Questions 1–5 about the situation. Each question helps the students focus on the feelings of the people involved in the activity, or explore other possible outcomes that could arise from the story.

The stories target a variety of social skills. They will increase students' overall social language development. The stories also target other important language skills: cause and effect, reasoning, sequencing, story retelling, paraphrasing, main idea, narrative form, answering questions, making inferences, drawing conclusions and outcome prediction, logical thinking, and analytical thinking.

The stories should appeal to a variety of students and easily adapt to a broad range of age groups. I recommend them for any student with social language dysfunction. They are excellent for students with Asperger's syndrome, PDD, autism, and severe language disorders. (However, the stories target a wide array of language skills, and are not limited to use with social skill deficits only.)

Deena E. Mahler

Suggested Ideas and Activities

Here are some fun ways to use these *Fold and Say® Social Skills* stories.

- Choose any story that fits the social situation you would like to teach/talk about. Make a copy. Read it to your students, and have them follow the directions on pages 3 and 4 of the story books.

- Send a story home that you reviewed in class for follow-up reinforcement.

- Choose one story as a topic for group discussion.

- Choose one story for each child in the group, and have each child discuss his or her story with the rest of the group.

- Use one story with a child in a one-on-one session.

- Prior to reading the story, cover the words and discuss what appears to be happening in the picture. Have the students discuss what they see. Encourage them to formulate their own stories. Then, read the story, and have the children brainstorm about it. Ask questions and have a group discussion.

- Try to incorporate the stories as part of a language or reading lesson.

- Use descriptive words to explain each character's emotions. Ask what else might make someone feel that way. Use many open-ended and "why" type of questions that best suit your students' abilities. Encourage development of higher, more mature thinking skills.

- Discuss the story. Have the students retell the story in their own words. Cover up the story and talk about what happened first, next, and last, using lots of transition words to challenge your students' sequencing skills.

- Relate the story to your students' own personal experiences. Ask questions such as, "Has this ever happened to you or someone you know?" Encourage students to share their experiences with the group. Were their experiences similar or different? How? Compare and contrast the experience with the story from the book.

- Ask the questions that follow the story, and note new questions that might arise during the discussion for use with another session.

- Draw on your students' ability to focus on the main idea. Ask them to make-up a sentence that best tells what the story was about.

- Have the students, either independently or as a group, draw, write, or tell what they think should be the conclusion of the story.

- Change the outcome of the story and discuss what could have happened instead. Formulate ideas on what elements could have made the situation different.

- Have the students act out the story in a mini-play, using lots of pretending. Have the students switch roles so they can see from the other character's perspective/point of view. Brainstorm about how each child feels and thinks in that role.

- When sending the story home for practice after that day's session, ask the student to retell the story to a family member.

- If a student has difficulty generalizing a targeted social skill, use a story that reminds that child about the target skill. Post it in a location where it will encourage and foster the new behavior.

Table of Contents
School Situations

Classroom 2–39
    Saying the Pledge of Allegiance 2
    It Was an Accident 3
    Asking for Directions 4
    It Wasn't Me 5
    Not Listening to the Teacher 6
    Letting Someone Finish 7
    Being a Helper 8
    Someone Feeling Jealous 9
    Making a Good Grade 10
    Having a Substitute Teacher 11
    Complimenting Someone 12
    A Helping Hand 13
    What Were the Directions 14
    That's Mine 15
    Not Feeling Good 16
    A Little Different Than Me 17
    Welcoming Someone 18
    Not Waiting Your Turn 19
    No Thank You 20
    Waiting to Talk 21
    Borrowing Someone's Things 22
    Making Something for Someone 23
    Giving a Holiday Gift 24
    Accidentally Tripping Someone 25
    Not Having Your Way 26
    Hoping Someone Gets Better Soon 27
    Having a Student Teacher 28
    A Friend Returns to School 29
    A Fire Drill 30
    Borrowing Something 31
    Cutting in Line 32
    Helping Someone 33
    Another Way of Talking 34
    Guess What I Did! 35
    Wanting to Ask a Question 36
    Please Stop It 37
    Choosing Partners 38
    Feeling Unhappy 39

School Hallway 40–45
    Meeting a Person Who is Blind 40
    Where Do I Belong? 41
    Finding Something 42
    Good Job 43
    No Talking in Line 44
    Walking on the Mopped Floor 45

School Bus 46–49
    Wanting to Ride the Bus 46
    Helping Pick Up 47
    How Was Your Day? 48
    Missing the Bus 49

Cafeteria 50–55
    Spilling on Someone 50
    Trading 51
    Being Overlooked 52
    Losing a Tooth 53
    Not Eating Politely 54
    May I Have Them? 55

Library 56–60
    Losing Something 56
    Not Talking Quietly 57
    Needing Help 58
    Checking Out a Book 59
    No Singing in the Library 60

Recess 61–75
    Please Stop Chasing Me 61
    Protecting Someone 62
    Telling Someone to Be Careful 63
    Finding Something 64
    Looking For a Friend to Play With 65
    Needing Help to Open 66
    Being in the Way 67
    Helping Someone Who is Hurt 68
    Not Looking 69
    Not Being Safe 70
    Being a Friend 71
    No Recess Time 72
    Someone is Pushing 73
    Needing Someone's Help 74
    Playing Together 75

Field Trip 76–78
    Staying with the Group 76
    Someone Asks Something 77
    Sharing a Seat 78

Table of Contents
Home & Community Situations

At Home with Family 80–111
Helping Your Mom with Laundry 80
Writing a Thank You Note 81
Asking if a Friend Can Come Over 82
Going on an Errand 83
Sending a Birthday Card 84
Sending a Get Well Card 85
Remembering Mom's Birthday 86
Wearing the Wrong Clothes 87
Keeping A Secret 88
Giving to the Needy 89
Making a Poor Choice 90
Embarrassing Someone 91
Showing Love 92
Not Right Now 93
Helping Mom Cook 94
Cleaning Up Your Room 95
Doing All of Your Chores 96
Closing the Door 97
Putting Toys Where They Belong 98
Letting Someone Rest 99
Forgetting Something 100
Dad is Going on a Trip 101
Making Something Special 102
When Dad is Working 103
Wanting to Stay Up Later 104
Having a Bad Dream 105
Grandmother Asks for Help 106
Meeting the New Babysitter 107
Getting the Same Gift Twice 108
Sliding Down the Banister 109
Finishing Work First 110
Being Invited Over 111

Brother/Sister 112–118
Mom Is Busy 112
Both Wanting the Same Thing 113
Someone Else's Party 114
Sitting in the Front 115
Someone Wants Your Toy 116
Privacy 117
Using Party Manners 118

Asking for Help 119–123
Getting Scared 119
I Can't Reach It 120
Excuse Me 121
I Need to Tell Someone 122
Needing Help to Zip 123

Telephone Manners 124–127
Sorry, Wrong Number 124
Answering the Phone for Someone 125
Interrupting 126
Taking a Message for Someone 127

In the Store 128–138
Staying with a Grown Up 128
Getting a Treat 129
Meeting Mom's Friend 130
Not Liking Something 131
Getting Lost 132
Making a Mess 133
Going Shopping with Mom 134
Not Getting What You Wanted to Buy ... 135
Introducing People 136
Not Staring 137
It's Not Mine 138

Table of Contents
Home & Community Situations

Restaurant **139–142**
- Eating Politely in a Restaurant 139
- Saying "No, Thank You" 140
- What About Me? 141
- Wanting Something Different 142

Talking to Adults **143–149**
- Feeling Good 143
- Sneezing 144
- Answering Someone 145
- Telling About Your Vacation 146
- Shaking Hands 147
- Getting a Gift 148
- Going In 149

Out with Family **150–165**
- When Someone Does a Mean Thing 150
- Not Wanting to Go Anymore 151
- Waiting Patiently 152
- Not Wanting to Do What Everyone Else Wants to Do 153
- Picking Up a Relative 154
- Watching for Cars 155
- Seeing Someone's New Baby 156
- Holding a Baby 157
- Giving Up Your Seat 158
- Visiting at the Hospital 159
- It's Time to Go 160
- Giving to Someone Younger 161
- Someone Is Scared 162
- Asking Permission 163
- Being Careful 164
- Being Proud 165

At the Doctor **166–168**
- Cooperating 166
- Being Good at the Doctor's 167
- Being Afraid of the Doctor 168

Out with Friends **169–206**
- Taking Too Much 169
- Deciding Where to Go 170
- Wanting to Do Something Different 171
- Seeing Someone You Know 172
- Seeing Someone's New Present 173
- Not Having Enough Information 174
- Putting Things Where They Belong 175
- Standing Too Close 176
- Saying Thanks 177
- Someone Has A New Baby 178
- Not Winning 179
- Hearing Someone Tease 180
- Helping Out 181
- Doing Something Different 182
- Asking to Share 183
- Not Being Nice 184
- Being Nice in the Water 185
- I'm Sorry You're Sad 186
- Asking for More Information 187
- Feeling Disappointed 188
- When Someone is Moving 189
- Not Making the Team 190
- Getting a Ride Home 191
- Wanting More 192
- When A Friend Isn't There 193
- Being Left Out 194
- Someone Wants to Take Something 195
- Being Afraid 196
- Needing to Stop 197
- Meeting Someone Who Is Special 198
- Wearing the Same Costume 199
- Going to a Party 200
- It's Not Funny 201
- Needing Something 202
- Saying "Happy Birthday" 203
- Going First 204
- Choosing Nicely 205
- Getting A Compliment 206

Certificates/Awards **207–210**

Blank Fold & Say® Booklets **211–212**

Parent/Helper Letter

Date:_____

Dear Parent/Helper:

    We are working on improving your child's ability to understand and problem solve in familiar social situations. You can help with your child's progress by doing these activities at home.

    Please complete the activities with a ✓ in the box(es).

- ❏ Read the story and have your child answer the questions.

- ❏ Read the story and have your child draw and/or write appropriate reaction/words to the situation.

- ❏ Ask your child to come up with a second appropriate response to each situation.

- ❏ Use the blank *Fold and Say*® page to encourage your child to write his/her own social situation. Your child may also draw pictures or use photos from a magazine.

- ❏ _____

Thank you for your support!

_____   _____
Name   Parent/Helper

Parent/Helper Letter

Date:_____

Dear Parent/Helper:

Your child is working on the following social skills:

❏ School Social Situations.

❏ Home Social Situations.

❏ Community Social Situations.

❏ _____.

Please read the attached story and have your child complete pages 3 and 4 of the story book.

❏ Please return by _____.

❏ You do not need to return the story to me.

_____   _____
Name   Parent/Helper

Saying the Pledge of Allegiance

The announcements come on in Tom's class in the morning. The principal says, "Now please stand for the pledge of allegiance."

Draw and/or write what happens next.

1. What should Tom do next?

2. Why do kids say the pledge of allegiance?

3. How should you act during the pledge?

4. What should you do during the pledge?

5. What should you not do during the pledge?

Steve wears his favorite shirt to school. Lisa sits on Steve's shirt by accident. Steve stands up. His shirt rips.

It Was an Accident

Draw and/or write what happens next.

1. Did Lisa mean to rip Steve's shirt?

2. What will Steve probably say or do next?

3. What will Lisa probably say to Steve?

4. Should Steve be angry with Lisa? Why or why not?

5. How could Steve get his shirt fixed?

Mr. Kennedy gives everyone a worksheet. Chris looks at the sheet. He doesn't know what to do.

Draw and/or write what happens next.

Asking for Directions

1. What should Chris do next?

2. Who would be the best person to help Chris?

3. What could Chris say to ask for help?

4. What will the teacher probably do then?

5. What should Chris say to the teacher after he gets help?

Mr. Maloney tells Sam to be quiet, but Sam wasn't talking.

Draw and/or write what happens next.

It Wasn't Me

1. What could Sam say to Mr. Maloney?

2. What might Mr. Maloney say?

3. What could Sam do so that this doesn't happen again?

4. What should Mr. Maloney do to make sure it doesn't happen again?

5. Has something like this ever happened to you? What did you do?

Sarah is talking to Brett while the teacher is talking. The teacher calls on Sarah to answer a question.

Draw and/or write what happens next.

Not Listening to the Teacher

1. Why didn't Sarah hear the teacher?

2. What should Sarah say now to the teacher?

3. What will the teacher probably say to Sarah?

4. What should Sarah do when the teacher is talking?

5. What should Brett do if Sarah tries to talk to him?

Tony is the clean-up helper today. He is throwing away the used paper towels. Sarah is still using her paper towels. She is still painting.

Letting Someone Finish

Draw and/or write what happens next.

1. What should Tony ask Sarah?

2. What will Sarah probably tell Tony?

3. What should Tony do since Sarah isn't finished?

4. How could Tony help Sarah?

5. What should Sarah do when she finishes her painting?

Chuck's teacher says, "Chuck, could you bring this to the office?"

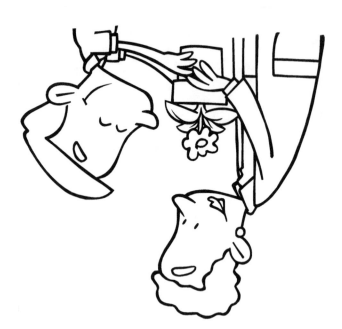

Draw and/or write what happens next.

Being a Helper

1. What should Chuck say to the teacher?

2. What will the teacher say if Chuck takes the item to the office?

3. How should Chuck act when he walks to the office?

4. What will Chuck say to the people working in the office when he gets there?

5. What should Chuck do after he leaves the office?

Zack got a low score on his reading test. Kari made an "A." Zack makes a sad face.

Draw and/or write what happens next.

Someone Feeling Jealous

1. Why is Zack making a sad face?

2. What does "jealous" mean?

3. How does Kari feel?

4. What could Kari say to Zack to help Zack feel better?

5. What could Zack have done instead of making a face?

Bobby gets all of the words right on his spelling test. Ms. Petersen hands Bobby his paper and smiles.

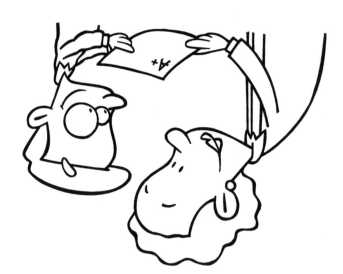

Draw and/or write what happens next.

Making a Good Grade

1. What will Ms. Petersen probably say to Bobby?

2. How will it make Bobby feel?

3. What could Bobby say to Ms. Petersen?

4. How will Bobby feel about being prepared for his spelling tests?

5. Why will Bobby feel that way?

Having a Substitute Teacher

Molly is in class. Her teacher is not there. A different lady wearing a name tag is in her class today. She starts to talk to Molly's class.

Draw and/or write what happens next.

1. Who is the lady?

2. What will the lady be doing all day?

3. What is she going to tell Molly's class?

4. Why is the lady wearing a name tag?

5. How should Molly's class treat the lady?

Mrs. Jordan's hair was very, very long on Friday. Monday it was very short.

Complimenting Someone

Draw and/or write what happens next.

1. What would be a nice thing for Austin to say to Mrs. Jordan when he sees her Monday morning?

2. How would it make Mrs. Jordan feel?

3. What will Mrs. Jordan probably say to Austin?

4. What should Austin NOT say to Mrs. Jordan?

5. Why should he NOT say that?

Mr. Barton is walking down the hall. He is carrying lots of things. Mr. Barton keeps dropping his papers. Jenny sees Mr. Barton.

Draw and/or write what happens next.

A Helping Hand

1. What should Jenny do next?

2. Why should Jenny do something?

3. What could she say to Mr. Barton?

4. What will Mr. Barton probably say to Jenny?

5. How will Jenny make Mr. Barton feel?

Ashley's teacher is telling the class which page to turn to. Ashley doesn't hear the teacher.

What Were the Directions?

Draw and/or write what happens next.

1. What should Ashley do next?

2. What should she ask her teacher?

3. What will the teacher tell her?

4. What will Ashley do after she hears the directions?

5. What could Ashley do the next time so she doesn't miss hearing the directions?

Jeff dropped his favorite pencil and lost it. A week later Jeff sees Benjamin writing with Jeff's pencil.

Draw and/or write what happens next.

That's Mine

1. How did Benjamin get Jeff's pencil?

2. How does Jeff feel seeing Benjamin with his pencil?

3. What should Jeff say to Benjamin if he wants the pencil back?

4. What could Benjamin say to Jeff?

5. Who could they talk with to help them solve this problem?

Ryan is in class. He is not feeling well.

Not Feeling Good

Draw and/or write what happens next.

1. Who should Ryan talk to?

2. Why should he talk to this person?

3. What will he tell this person?

4. What might this person say to Ryan?

5. What will Ryan probably do next?

Komoko is from Japan. Komoko is in Jamie's class. Komoko doesn't speak English very well, and she doesn't look like Jamie. Jamie doesn't know why.

A Little Different Than Me

Draw and/or write what happens next.

1. Why does Komoko look different?

2. Is it okay that Komoko looks different?

3. Could Jamie be Komoko's friend?

4. What could Jamie do to learn more about Komoko?

5. How would Komoko feel if no one wanted to be her friend?

Clint and his classmates are sitting down. Mr. Stillman says, "Boys and girls, this is Ricky. Ricky's family moved here last week."

Draw and/or write what happens next.

Welcoming Someone

1. How does Ricky feel? Why?

2. What should Clint say to Ricky?

3. When should Clint talk to Ricky?

4. How will Ricky feel if Clint talks to him?

5. What can the other kids in the class do for Ricky?

Maria is talking to Miss Greta. Kyle starts to talk to Miss Greta at the same time.

Not Waiting Your Turn

Draw and/or write what happens next.

1. What is Kyle doing that he shouldn't be doing? Why?

2. What will Miss Greta probably say to Kyle? Why?

3. What should Kyle do now?

4. What should Kyle do the next time someone else is talking first?

5. Why should Kyle do that?

Sam brings cupcakes for the whole class. He hands one to Kerri. Kerri doesn't want a cupcake.

Draw and/or write what happens next.

No Thank You

1. What should Kerri say to Sam?

2. What could Sam say back?

3. What could Sam do with the cupcake?

4. What could Sam say to the class to find out who wants a cupcake?

5. What could the class say to Sam for bringing the cupcakes?

Josh and his classmates are all talking to Mrs. Raphael at the same time. Josh is asking, "Can I get some water?" over and over to Mrs. Raphael.

Waiting to Talk

Draw and/or write what happens next.

1. What is Josh doing that he shouldn't be doing?

2. What should all of the kids be doing instead of talking at the same time?

3. Why shouldn't the kids all talk at the same time?

4. How many times should Josh ask for something?

5. What will Mrs. Raphael probably say to the kids and Josh?

David borrows Pedro's favorite pencil. He is playing drums with it on his desk. The pencil breaks.

Draw and/or write what happens next.

Borrowing Someone's Things

1. How does David feel?

2. What is David going to tell Pedro?

3. What will Pedro probably say?

4. What could David do to make things better?

5. How will Pedro feel then?

It is the end of the year. Karla hands Mrs. Bice a picture of herself. It says, "Mrs. Bice, you are a very nice teacher. I'm glad you were my teacher. Love, Karla."

Making Something for Someone

Draw and/or write what happens next.

1. What will Mrs. Bice say to Karla?

2. What might Mrs. Bice do next?

3. What does Mrs. Bice think of Karla's picture?

4. What will Mrs. Bice do with the picture?

5. What words did Karla write that made Mrs. Bice happy?

It is Valentine's Day. Danny hands Ms. Reece a box of chocolates.

Giving a Holiday Gift

Draw and/or write what happens next.

1. What will Ms. Reece say to Danny?

2. What will Danny say to his teacher?

3. How did Danny make her feel? Why?

4. How does Danny feel about his teacher?

5. Why do we give gifts to people?

Kelly is standing on Lilliana's shoestring. Lilliana starts to walk.

Accidentally Tripping Someone

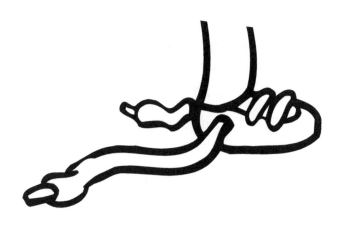

Draw and/or write what happens next.

1. What will probably happen to Lilliana?

2. What should Kelly do next?

3. What should Kelly NOT do?

4. What should Kelly say to Lilliana?

5. How will Lilliana feel when Kelly says that?

Mr. Peterman is handing out lollipops. Heather says she wants a red one. Mr. Peterman says that Rochelle got the last red lollipop.

Draw and/or write what happens next.

Not Having Your Way

1. How does Heather feel?

2. What should Heather say?

3. What might Mr. Peterman say to Heather?

4. What should Heather NOT say?

5. Why should Heather NOT say that?

#BK-293 204 Fold & Say® Social Stories • ©2002 Super Duper® Publications
www.superduperinc.com • 1-800-277-8737

Hoping Someone Gets Better Soon

Zack and Toby are talking. Toby asks Zack if he wants to come over and play after school. Zack says he has to go visit his mom in the hospital tonight and can't go to Toby's house.

Draw and/or write what happens next.

1. What should Toby say to Zack?

2. How will that make Zack feel?

3. What could Zack say to Toby?

4. What could Toby do for Zack?

5. How might that make Zack feel?

Craig's teacher tells the class that they will have a student teacher for a little while. His teacher says that the student teacher is going to college to learn to become a real teacher.

Draw and/or write what happens next.

Having a Student Teacher

1. Why is the student teacher in the classroom?

2. How should the kids treat the student teacher?

3. What could the kids say to the student teacher when they meet her?

4. How will that make the student teacher feel?

5. What might the student teacher help the kids learn?

Luis had to get his tonsils out and wasn't at school for a while. Missy is very glad that Luis is back at school.

Draw and/or write what happens next.

A Friend Returns to School

1. What might Missy say to Luis?

2. How will that make Luis feel?

3. What could Luis say to Missy and the other children?

4. How might Luis feel about returning to school?

5. What may the teacher say to Luis?

Jessie's teacher tells the class that they have to practice for a fire drill. Jessie gets very scared and asks the teacher if there is really a fire at school.

Draw and/or write what happens next.

A Fire Drill

1. What will the teacher probably say to Jessie?

2. What might Jessie say to the teacher?

3. Does Jessie need to be afraid of the fire drill?

4. Why is the teacher telling the kids they need to practice for the fire drill?

5. How will Jessie feel about a fire drill after she practices?

Katie doesn't have a pencil. Jeff has three pencils. Katie needs to borrow one from Jeff.

Borrowing Something

1. How should Katie ask Jeff for one of his pencils?

2. What may Jeff say?

3. What should Katie say if Jeff says, "Yes"?

4. What should Katie say if Jeff says "No"?

5. What type of things do you share?

Draw and/or write what happens next.

The kids are lined up to wash their hands before going to lunch. Jim pushes and shoves and tries to get ahead in the line.

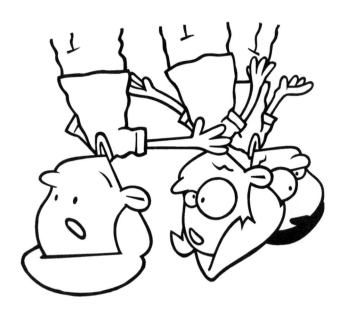

Draw and/or write what happens next.

Cutting in Line

1. What will the other children probably say to Jim?

2. How do the other kids feel about Jim pushing and shoving them?

3. What could happen if a child pushes Jim?

4. What should Jim say to the other kids?

5. What should Jim do instead of pushing and shoving?

Jonathan drops his book on the floor. Ken sees him drop it.

Helping Someone

Draw and/or write what happens next.

1. What should Ken do next?

2. Why should Ken do something?

3. What will Ken say to Jonathan?

4. What will Jonathan say to Ken?

5. How will Jonathan feel when Ken helps him?

Ian walks up to Leonard, a boy sitting in a wheelchair. Leonard pushes a button attached to a machine that says, "Hi. My name is Leonard."

Another Way of Talking

Draw and/or write what happens next.

1. What should Ian say next?

2. What should Ian NOT say?

3. What is something Ian should NOT do?

4. If Ian says hello too, how will that make Leonard feel?

5. Why doesn't Leonard use his mouth to talk?

It is Monday. Mr. Jackson asks Casey if she had a good weekend. Mr. Jackson doesn't know that Casey went to the zoo yesterday.

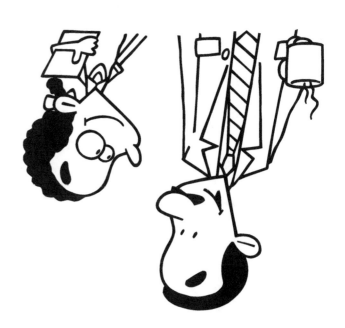

Guess What I Did?

Draw and/or write what happens next.

1. What will Casey say to Mr. Jackson?

2. What will Mr. Jackson say back to Casey?

3. What might Casey say about the zoo?

4. What questions might Mr. Jackson ask Casey?

5. Will Casey ask Mr. Jackson about his weekend?

Brandon and his class are listening to the people from the zoo talk about the animals they brought to school. Brandon wants to ask a question about the iguana.

Draw and/or write what happens next.

Wanting to Ask a Question

1. What should Brandon do to let the people know he has a question?

2. When should Brandon ask his question?

3. What should Brandon NOT do when it is time for his question?

4. What question might Brandon ask about the iguana?

5. What should Brandon say after the people answer his question?

Ellie and her fellow classmates are in music class. Bethany keeps shaking the tambourine in Ellie's face.

Draw and/or write what happens next.

Please Stop It

1. What is Bethany doing wrong?

2. How is she making Ellie feel?

3. What might Ellie say to Bethany?

4. What should Bethany do after Ellie talks with her?

5. Who could Ellie get to help her if Bethany does not listen to her?

Choosing Partners

Abby asks Skye to be her partner for the game in P.E. class. Skye already has a partner.

1. What will Skye probably say to Abby?

2. How will this make Abby feel?

3. What could Abby say to Skye?

4. What should Abby do next?

5. Who could Abby talk to if she can't find a partner?

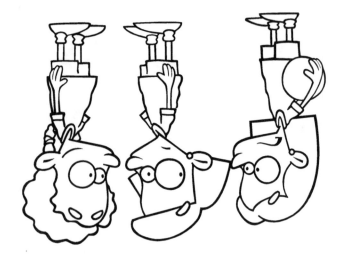

Draw and/or write what happens next.

Evan gets home from school. He looks sad. His mom and dad ask him what's wrong. Evan says that one of the kids called him names at school.

Draw and/or write what happens next.

Feeling Unhappy

1. What could Evan's parents tell Evan to make him feel better?

2. What might Evan say to his parents?

3. Will Evan talk to the other kids at school about the name calling?

4. Who could help Evan talk to the kids at school?

5. Why should people not call each other names?

Billy sees a girl walking down the hall with a cane. She moves the cane back and forth on the floor. Billy goes up to the girl and asks, "Why do you have a cane?"

Meeting a Person Who Is Blind

Draw and/or write what happens next.

1. What is the first thing Billy should have asked the girl?

2. What was the girl doing with the cane?

3. What will she probably tell Billy?

4. Could Billy be her friend even though he doesn't use a cane?

5. How could you help a blind person at school?

Where Do I Belong?

Carrie leaves the class. She is washing her hands in the bathroom. The fire alarm rings while she is in the bathroom.

Draw and/or write what happens next.

1. Where will Carrie's class go next? Why?

2. What should Carrie do?

3. How will Carrie know where to go?

4. What should Carrie do if she isn't sure where to go?

5. How should you act during a fire drill?

Peter is walking down the hall. He finds a ribbon that he saw Katie wearing earlier that day.

Draw and/or write what happens next.

Finding Something

1. Whose ribbon does Peter think he found?

2. How does he know who owns the ribbon?

3. What should Peter do with the ribbon?

4. What will he say to Katie?

5. What might Katie say to Peter?

Krissy's class is walking down the hall. They are very quiet. Mrs. Winchester smiles and talks to them.

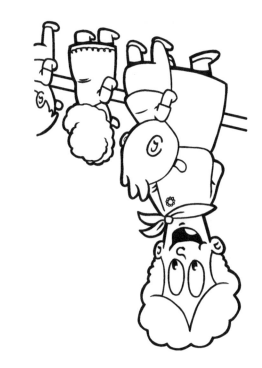

Draw and/or write what happens next.

Good Job

1. Why is the class being quiet in the hallway?

2. What is Mrs. Winchester probably going to say?

3. Why will she say that to them?

4. What is Krissy's class doing that is good?

5. How will Krissy's class feel after Mrs. Winchester talks to them?

The school rule is, "No talking in line." Marcus keeps turning around to talk to Harry.

Draw and/or write what happens next.

No Talking in Line

1. What should Harry say to Marcus?

2. Why should Harry say this?

3. What could happen if Marcus keeps talking to Harry?

4. How would Harry feel then?

5. What should Marcus do after Harry asks him to stop talking to him?

©2002 Super Duper® Publications

Mrs. Hewitt is mopping the floor at school. She left a dry path on the side for the kids to walk. Shannon isn't looking and she walks on the part that Mrs. Hewitt is mopping. Mrs. Hewitt looks sad.

Walking on the Mopped Floor

©2002 Super Duper® Publications

Draw and/or write what happens next.

1. Why does Mrs. Hewitt look sad?

2. Why did Mrs. Hewitt want Shannon to walk on the side?

3. What might Mrs. Hewitt say to Shannon?

4. What should Shannon say to Mrs. Hewitt?

5. What should Shannon do the next time?

Jason's mom drives Jason to school every day in their car. Jason wants to ride the bus to school instead.

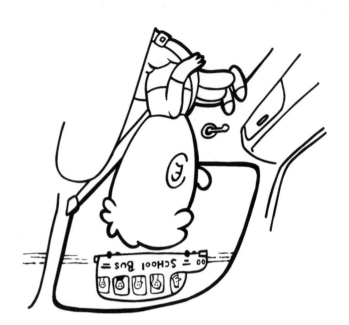

Wanting to Ride the Bus

1. Why does Jason want to ride the bus?

2. How could Jason tell his mom he wants to ride the bus?

3. What might his mom say?

4. How will Jason feel if his mom says, "No"?

5. How will Jason feel if his mom says, "Okay"?

Draw and/or write what happens next.

Keaton gets off the bus. Lindsay is behind her. Keaton's bag suddenly opens. All of her things fall on the ground.

Helping Pick Up

Draw and/or write what happens next.

1. How does Keaton feel?

2. What should Lindsay do? Why?

3. Why should Lindsay do something?

4. What will Keaton probably say to Lindsay?

5. How will this make Lindsay feel?

Gordon gets off the school bus. His dad is waiting for him. Gordon's dad looks at Gordon and smiles.

How Was Your Day?

Draw and/or write what happens next.

1. What will Gordon's dad probably ask Gordon?

2. Why is Gordon's dad asking Gordon this question?

3. What is something Gordon might say to his dad?

4. How will Gordon's dad feel if Gordon does not answer him?

5. How does Gordon feel when his dad asks about his day?

©2002 Super Duper® Publications

Paula walks outside to catch the bus, but she sees the bus drive away.

Draw and/or write what happens next.

©2002 Super Duper® Publications

Missing the Bus

1. Why is the bus leaving?

2. What is one reason why Paula might have missed the bus?

3. What could Paula do next?

4. What could she say to her mom or dad?

5. What will they probably do next?

Spilling on Someone

Aaron and Elizabeth are waiting in line to put away their lunch trays. Rashad bumps into Aaron by accident. Aaron's tray spills on Elizabeth's new dress.

Draw and/or write what happens next.

1. What should Aaron say to Elizabeth?

2. What should Rashad say to Aaron and Elizabeth?

3. What might Elizabeth say to them?

4. Should Aaron be angry at Rashad?

5. How will Elizabeth feel?

Trading

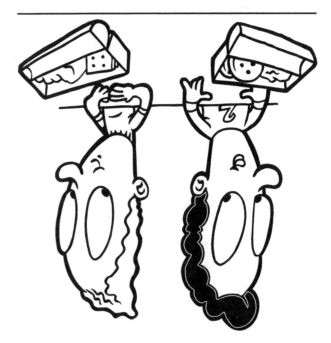

Michael is sitting next to Peter in the cafeteria. Peter asks Michael if he can have some of Michael's cookies. Michael sees that Peter has Michael's favorite kind of crackers in his lunchbox.

Draw and/or write what happens next.

1. What might Michael ask Peter?

2. What could Peter say?

3. What might the boys end up doing?

4. How will this make both of the boys feel?

5. Why do people "trade" things?

Ravi is in the cafeteria. Ms. Raynah is serving food to the kids. Ms. Raynah forgets to put juice on Ravi's tray.

Draw and/or write what happens next.

Being Overlooked

1. How does Ravi feel?

2. What should Ravi do or say?

3. What will Ms. Raynah probably say to Ravi?

4. What will Ms. Raynah do next?

5. What should Ravi do if Ms. Raynah does not have any more juice?

Allison is eating a roll in the cafeteria. Her tooth falls out and her mouth is bleeding a little.

Losing a Tooth

Draw and/or write what happens next.

1. How does Allison feel?

2. What could Allison do next?

3. Why did Allison's tooth fall out?

4. Should Allison worry about her mouth bleeding?

5. What might Allison tell her parents when she gets home from school?

Jessie is sitting next to John in the cafeteria. Jessie is opening his mouth very wide and showing John his food after he chews it up. John does not like that and he wants Jessie to stop.

Draw and/or write what happens next.

Not Eating Politely

1. What could John say to Jessie?

2. What should Jessie do after that?

3. What could John do if Jessie won't stop?

4. Who could help John get Jessie to stop?

5. What should people do with their mouths and lips when they are eating?

Alexander doesn't want his peas. Kira loves peas. Kira is still very hungry.

Draw and/or write what happens next.

May I Have Them?

1. What does Kira want?

2. What might Kira ask Alexander?

3. What could Alexander say to Kira?

4. How will Alexander feel if Kira eats his peas?

5. What should Kira and Alexander do when they are finished eating?

Losing Something

Kevin looks in his desk for the library book that he checked out from the library. It isn't there.

1. How does Kevin feel?

2. What can Kevin do next?

3. Who should he talk to?

4. What might he say?

5. What will his teacher or the librarian probably say to him?

Draw and/or write what happens next.

It is silent reading time in the library. Sam is talking very loudly to Sally, who is trying to read.

Not Talking Quietly

Draw and/or write what happens next.

1. What should Sally say to Sam?

2. What is Sam doing that is not following the rule?

3. Why does Sam keep talking to Sally?

4. What should Sam do after Sally tells him how she feels?

5. What should Sally do if Sam keeps talking?

Desmond is in the library. He can't find the book he wants.

Needing Help

1. What should Desmond do to get help?

2. What would Desmond say to the librarian?

3. What would the librarian probably do?

4. What should Desmond say after the librarian helps him find the book?

5. What should Desmond do if the library does not have the book?

Draw and/or write what happens next.

Jack went to the library. He wants to bring home a book that he found in the library.

Checking Out a Book

Draw and/or write what happens next.

1. What should Jack do next?

2. Who should he go talk to?

3. What should Jack say to the librarian?

4. What will the librarian say?

5. What will happen after that?

Layla is in the school library. She is singing. The librarian walks over to Layla.

No Singing in the Library

Draw and/or write what happens next.

1. What will the librarian probably say to Layla?

2. Why is she going to talk to Layla?

3. What should Layla do after the librarian talks to her?

4. How should people act at the library? Why?

5. Why should they act this way in the library?

#BK-293 204 Fold & Say® Social Stories • ©2002 Super Duper® Publications
www.superduperinc.com • 1-800-277-8737

Robert is chasing James during recess. James doesn't want to be chased.

Draw and/or write what happens next.

Please Stop Chasing Me

1. Why doesn't James want to be chased?

2. What should James say to Robert?

3. What should Robert do after that?

4. What should James do if Robert doesn't stop?

5. What should James NOT do to get Robert to stop chasing him?

Cedric is talking to Celia during recess. She has a spider in her hair but she doesn't know it.

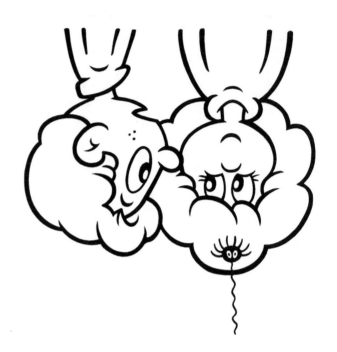

Draw and/or write what happens next.

Protecting Someone

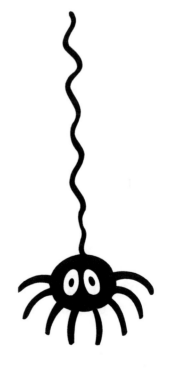

1. What should Cedric say and do next?

2. Why should Cedric tell Celia about the spider?

3. What might happen if Cedric doesn't tell Celia about the spider?

4. How will Celia feel about Cedric telling her about the spider?

5. What will Celia say to Cedric after he tells her about the spider?

Tara sees a log on the ground. Her friend Mark is running and doesn't see the log up ahead.

Telling Someone to Be Careful

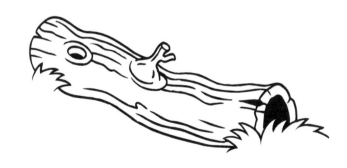

Draw and/or write what happens next.

1. What could happen if Tara doesn't tell Mark about the log?

2. What should Tara tell Mark?

3. What will Mark do then?

4. What should Mark say to Tara?

5. How will Tara feel if she doesn't tell Mark about the log?

Recess is over. It is time to go in. Ben sees John's coat lying on the ground, but John is already back inside.

Draw and/or write what happens next.

Finding Something

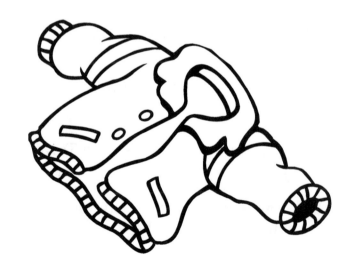

1. Why is John's coat still outside?

2. What should Ben do with John's coat?

3. Why should someone bring John's coat inside?

4. What will John probably say when he gets his coat back?

5. How will Ben feel when John says that?

David says to the teacher, "I don't have anybody to play with."

Draw and/or write what happens next.

Looking For a Friend to Play With

1. How does David feel?

2. What could the teacher tell David?

3. What could David do?

4. How would he ask someone to play with him?

5. What may the other person say when David asks him or her to play?

It is snack time during recess. Noah is having trouble opening his pack of crackers.

Draw and/or write what happens next.

Needing Help to Open

1. What should Noah do?

2. How might he ask for help?

3. Who could he ask for help?

4. What will that person probably say?

5. What should Noah say afterwards?

#BK-293 204 Fold & Say® Social Stories • ©2002 Super Duper® Publications
www.superduperinc.com • 1-800-277-8737

Being in the Way

Cooper and Nathaniel are playing marbles on top of the hopscotch game. Lila and Teesha want to play hopscotch.

Draw and/or write what happens next.

1. What will the girls say to the boys?

2. What should the boys say?

3. What should the boys do?

4. Why should the boys do that?

5. What should the girls say when the boys do that?

Mia is crying. She is on the ground holding her knee. There is dirt on her. Jasmine sees Mia.

Draw and/or write what happens next.

Helping Someone Who is Hurt

1. What happened to Mia?

2. Why is she crying?

3. What could Jasmine say to Mia?

4. What might Jasmine do to help Mia?

5. How would Mia feel if Jasmine helps her?

Sondra is running. She is looking behind her. Rosa doesn't see Sondra. Sondra doesn't see Rosa.

Draw and/or write what happens next.

Not Looking

1. What is going to happen next?

2. What should Sondra say to Rosa?

3. What should Rosa say?

4. How can Sondra make Rosa feel better?

5. What should kids do when they're running?

There is a huge ant pile on the playground. Andrew and Avery look at the ant pile. Avery pushes a stick into the pile.

Not Being Safe

Draw and/or write what happens next.

1. What might happen next?

2. Why is it not safe to push a stick into an ant pile?

3. What should the boys do next?

4. What should the boys NOT do next?

5. What should Andrew say to Avery?

Being a Friend

Gloria is at recess. Gloria sees Jessica, the new girl in her class. It is her first day at Gloria's school. Jessica is standing alone. She is crying.

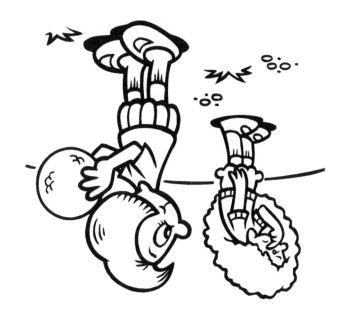

Draw and/or write what happens next.

1. Why is Jessica alone?

2. Why is she crying?

3. What could Gloria do next?

4. What might she say to Jessica?

5. How will Gloria's words make Jessica feel?

No Recess Time

Tasha asks Kayla if she wants to play basketball with her during recess. Kayla tells Tasha that she has to stay in during recess.

Draw and/or write what happens next.

1. How does Kayla feel?

2. What could Tasha say to Kayla now?

3. What may Kayla say back to Tasha?

4. What could Tasha do now to have a friend to play basketball with?

5. What will Kayla do next time to avoid being punished?

Someone is Pushing

It is recess time. The kids are going outside to play. A boy pushes Fletcher out of the door because he wants Fletcher to go faster.

Draw and/or write what happens next.

1. What will happen to Fletcher?

2. What should the boy have done instead?

3. How does Fletcher feel?

4. What could Fletcher say to the boy?

5. Why should children wait their turn and not push other kids?

Albert is trying to tie his shoelaces. He keeps trying but he can't do it.

Draw and/or write what happens next.

Needing Someone's Help

1. What could Albert do next?

2. Who should he talk to?

3. What will this person do after Albert talks with him?

4. What should Albert say after that?

5. How will Albert feel when that person helps him?

#BK-293 204 Fold & Say® Social Stories • ©2002 Super Duper® Publications
www.superduperinc.com • 1-800-277-8737

Abdul is standing alone on the playground. Hunter is alone, too. Abdul looks at Hunter. Abdul starts walking.

Playing Together

Draw and/or write what happens next.

1. Where is Abdul going?

2. Why is Abdul going over there?

3. What will Abdul probably say to Hunter?

4. What might Hunter say to Abdul?

5. How will both boys feel after they talk?

Staying with the Group

Crystal's class goes on a field trip to the zoo. Crystal sees a peacock in a field and starts walking toward it. She walks away from her group.

Draw and/or write what happens next.

1. What should Crystal be doing instead of going to see the peacock?

2. Why shouldn't Crystal go see the peacock?

3. What will the person in charge probably say to Crystal?

4. Why will this person talk with Crystal?

5. What will Crystal say to this person?

Someone Asks Something

Alicia's class went to the space station for a field trip. Alicia's class is ready to leave now. Mr. Hobson asks Alicia, "So, did you enjoy your trip here today?"

Draw and/or write what happens next.

1. What might Alicia say to Mr. Hobson?

2. What might Mr. Hobson say back to her?

3. What shouldn't Alicia say to Mr. Hobson?

4. Why shouldn't Alicia say that?

5. What else could Alicia say to Mr. Hobson?

Devin's class is going on a field trip to the space center. The kids are getting on the bus. Devin gets on the bus and sees his friend Kelly. Devin wants to sit next to Kelly.

Sharing a Seat

1. What does Devin want Kelly to do?

2. Why does Devin want to share a seat with Kelly?

3. What should Devin ask Kelly?

4. What do you think Kelly might say to Devin?

5. How will that make Devin feel?

Draw and/or write what happens next.

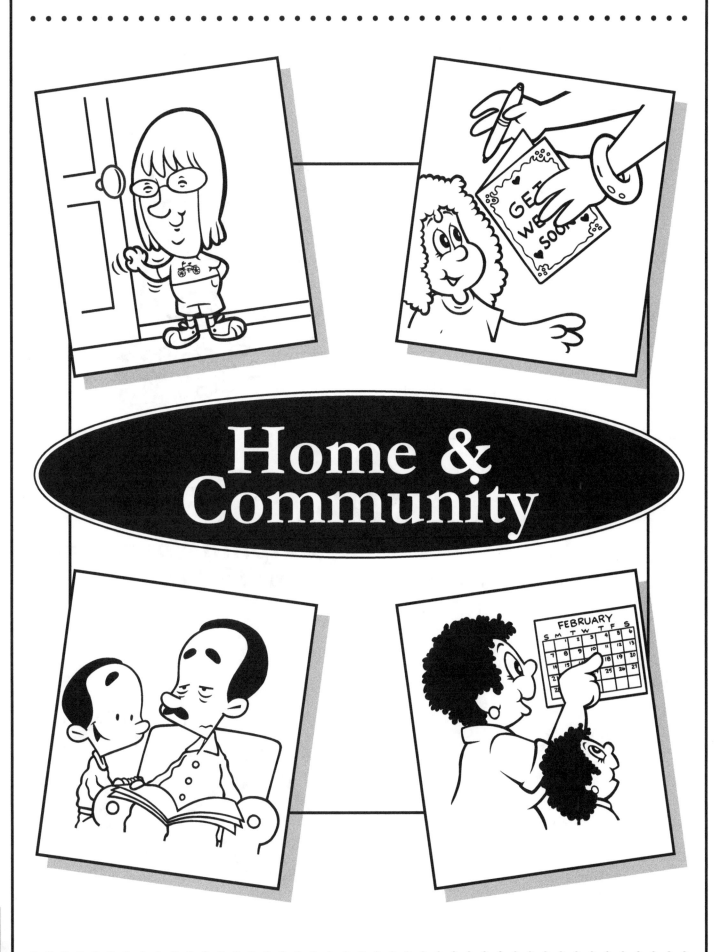

Helping Your Mom with Laundry

Tom's mom is trying to carry clean laundry that needs to be folded. Tom picks up the clothes that fall. He says, "I'll help you, mom."

Draw and/or write what happens next.

1. Why does Tom want to help his mom?

2. What will Tom's mom probably say to Tom?

3. How will Tom feel?

4. How will Tom's mom probably feel about Tom helping?

5. What other things could Tom do to help his mom?

Grace's grandma sent Grace some money for her birthday. Grace's mom says, "Let's send grandma a thank-you note."

Draw and/or write what happens next.

Writing a Thank-You Note

1. What should Grace say next?

2. What should Grace do next?

3. What words might Grace write in the note?

4. Why should Grace write a thank-you note?

5. How will Grace's grandma probably feel when she gets the note?

Asking If a Friend Can Come Over

Elliott wants his friend Paul to come over. Elliott needs to find out if he can ask Paul to come over.

Draw and/or write what happens next.

1. Who does Elliott need to talk to about Paul coming over?

2. What will Elliott say to this person?

3. What will Elliott do if this person says that Paul can come over?

4. Who does Paul need to talk to about going over to Elliott's?

5. What should Paul do if this person says, "No"?

Marcos' mom is cooking. She says to Marcos, "Marcos, I need you to go next door and ask Mrs. Johnson if we can have a cup of milk."

Draw and/or write what happens next.

Going On an Errand

1. What should Marcos say to his mom?

2. What should he do next?

3. What should Marcos say to Mrs. Johnson when he gets to her house?

4. What might Mrs. Johnson say?

5. What should Marcos say when Mrs. Johnson gives him the milk?

Selena's mom says that next Thursday is Grandpa's birthday. Selena asks, "Can I send Grandpa a birthday card?"

Draw and/or write what happens next.

Sending a Birthday Card

1. Why does Selena want to send her grandpa a card?

2. What will Selena's mom probably say?

3. What could Selena write in the card?

4. How will Selena's grandpa probably feel when he gets the card?

5. What will Selena's grandpa probably say to Selena when he reads the card?

Sarah's Aunt Claire is very old and sick. Sarah's mom says, "Sarah, please sign Aunt Claire's get-well card."

Draw and/or write what happens next.

Sending a Get-Well Card

1. What should Sarah say to her mom?

2. What should Sarah do next?

3. What is a get-well card?

4. Why do people send cards to people when they are sick?

5. Why would Aunt Claire like a get-well card?

Helen's mom's birthday is Saturday. Helen asks her dad if they can go to the store so Helen can buy her mom a present.

Remembering Mom's Birthday

Draw and/or write what happens next.

1. Why does Helen want to buy her mom a present?

2. What will Helen's dad probably say?

3. How will Helen's mom feel about Helen remembering her birthday?

4. What will Helen's mom say to Helen when she opens her gift?

5. How will Helen feel then?

It is snowing outside. Maria has on shorts and a T-shirt. Maria goes to open the front door. Her mom stops her before she can go outside.

Draw and/or write what happens next.

Wearing the Wrong Clothes

1. What is Maria's mom probably going to tell Maria?

2. Why is her mom going to say that?

3. What should Maria do next?

4. What might Maria say to her mom after she talks to her?

5. What types of clothes will Maria put on?

Gavin and his mom bought dad a new barbecue grill for his birthday. Gavin's mom said, "Gavin, don't tell Dad, because it's a secret." Gavin told his dad about the grill anyway.

Keeping a Secret

Draw and/or write what happens next.

1. How does Gavin's mom probably feel?

2. What did Gavin's mom probably say to Gavin after he told his dad the secret?

3. Why didn't Gavin's mom want Gavin to tell his dad about the grill?

4. How does Gavin probably feel about telling his dad?

5. When was Gavin's dad supposed to find out about the grill?

Trevor's mom says, "Trevor, we need to donate some of your old toys to a needy family."

Giving To the Needy

Draw and/or write what happens next.

1. What do "donate" and "needy" mean?

2. What does Trevor's mom want Trevor to do?

3. Why does Trevor's mom want to give some of his toys away?

4. What should Trevor say to his mom about donating his old toys?

5. How will the people who get the toys feel?

Isaiah picks most of the flowers from his mom's flower garden. He hands them to his mom, but she looks sad.

Draw and/or write what happens next.

Making a Poor Choice

1. Why does Isaiah's mom look sad?

2. What will Isaiah say to his mom?

3. What will she say to Isaiah?

4. Why will she say that?

5. What could Isaiah do next time instead?

Pamela's mom is talking to Mrs. Smith. Pamela's sister, Claire, puts a sticker on Pamela's back while Pamela's mom isn't looking.

Embarrassing Someone

Draw and/or write what happens next.

1. What should Pamela do when she finds out about the sticker?

2. What should Pamela say to her sister?

3. What will happen if Pamela and her sister start fighting?

4. How will Pamela's mom feel if they fight in front of Mrs. Smith?

5. What should Claire do next time?

Showing Love

Paul's mom tells Paul that she loves him. She gives Paul a big hug.

Draw and/or write what happens next.

1. What should Paul say next?

2. Why is Paul's mom telling him that she loves him?

3. How does this make Paul feel?

4. Why is Paul's mom giving him a hug?

5. What will Paul and his mom do next?

Not Right Now

Jonah's mom says its late and everyone needs to hurry. Jonah asks if he can get some juice to drink before they go.

©2002 Super Duper Publications

Draw and/or write what happens next.

1. What will Jonah's mom say about getting some juice?

2. Why will she say that?

3. Why should Jonah not ask for juice now?

4. When is a good time to ask for something?

5. What should Jonah do next time?

Nadia is watching cartoons. Her mom walks in from the kitchen. Nadia's mom says, "Nadia, will you come help me cook breakfast?"

Draw and/or write what happens next.

Helping Mom Cook

1. What should Nadia say to her mom?

2. Should Nadia go help her mom, even if she'd rather watch TV?

3. What will Nadia's mom probably say to Nadia if she helps?

4. How will Nadia's mom feel if Nadia helps her?

5. Why should Nadia help her mom?

Earlier this morning, Mark's dad asked Mark to clean up his room. Mark is finishing picking everything up. Mark's dad walks into the room.

Draw and/or write what happens next.

Cleaning Up Your Room

1. What did Mark's dad ask Mark to do?

2. What is Mark doing?

3. Did Mark listen to his dad?

4. Will Mark's dad be happy or sad?

5. What will Mark's dad probably say to Mark?

Jonathan has a chart for keeping track of doing his chores. Jonathan's dad is putting a star on Jonathan's chart for today's chores. Jonathan's chart has lots of star stickers on it.

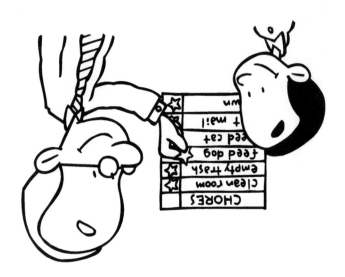

Draw and/or write what happens next.

Doing All of Your Chores

1. What is a "chore"?

2. Why do kids have chores?

3. Why is Jonathan's dad putting a star on the chart?

4. Why does Jonathan's chart have so many stars on it?

5. How does Jonathan probably feel when he sees all of his stars?

Roger walks in from playing in the snow outside. He leaves the front door open. Roger's dad walks by.

Closing the Door

1. What will Roger's dad probably say to him?

2. What should Roger say to his dad?

3. What should Roger do next?

4. What should people do to the door when they walk into a house?

5. Why should Roger close the door?

Draw and/or write what happens next.

Jessica left her toy on the stairs. Jessica's mom almost trips on the toy.

Draw and/or write what happens next.

Putting Toys Where They Belong

1. What will Jessica's mom probably say to Jessica?

2. What should Jessica say?

3. How does Jessica feel?

4. Where should Jessica keep her toys?

5. Why shouldn't Jessica keep her toys on the stairs?

©2002 Super Duper® Publications

Mom tells Scott that Daddy is sick. Scott walks over to his dad and asks if he wants to go upstairs and play with him.

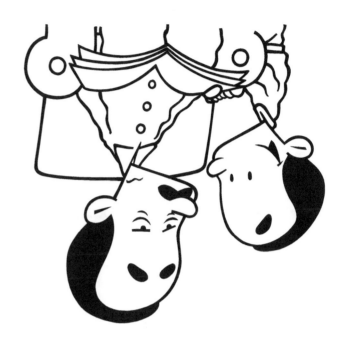

Letting Someone Rest

©2002 Super Duper® Publications

Draw and/or write what happens next.

1. What will Scott's dad probably tell Scott?

2. Why might Scott's dad not want to play right now?

3. Why should Scott let his dad rest?

4. What should Scott do instead of asking his dad to play?

5. When will Scott's dad feel like playing?

It is raining outside. Lianne is inside with her family. Suddenly, Lianne remembers that her shoes are outside.

Forgetting Something

Draw and/or write what happens next.

1. What does Lianne need to do?

2. What could happen to Lianne's shoes if they stay outside?

3. How will Lianne feel if her shoes get wet?

4. What should Lianne tell her mom or dad?

5. What will her mom or dad tell her?

Christopher's dad tells Christopher that he has to go out of town on a business trip.

Draw and/or write what happens next.

Dad is Going on a Trip

1. How does Christopher feel?

2. What might Christopher say to his dad?

3. What could Christopher ask his dad?

4. What might Christopher's dad say to Christopher?

5. What will Christopher's dad do before he goes on the trip?

It is Father's Day. Douglas hands his dad a picture that he drew. His dad smiles.

Draw and/or write what happens next.

Making Something Special for Someone

1. Why is Douglas' dad smiling?

2. What will Douglas' dad probably say to Douglas?

3. What will Douglas' dad probably do with the picture?

4. How will this make Douglas feel?

5. How did the picture make Douglas' dad feel?

Tawnia's dad said, "You kids need to play so I can finish some work that is due, okay?" Then he shut the door.

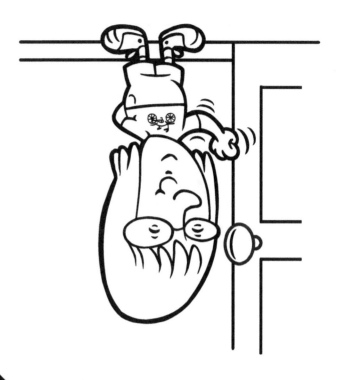

Draw and/or write what happens next.

When Dad Is Working

1. What did Tawnia's dad tell the kids to go do?

2. Why doesn't Tawnia's dad want to play with the kids now?

3. What should Tawnia go do?

4. How will Tawnia's dad feel about her knocking on the door?

5. What might Tawnia's dad say to her when he opens the door?

It is nighttime. Weston's parents tell him to go to bed. Weston says, "But I don't want to go to bed. None of my friends go to bed so early."

Wanting to Stay Up Later

Draw and/or write what happens next.

1. How does Weston feel?

2. What will Weston's parents probably tell him?

3. What should he say?

4. What should Weston do next?

5. Why should Weston do that?

Evie had a bad dream. She is scared. She goes into her parent's room.

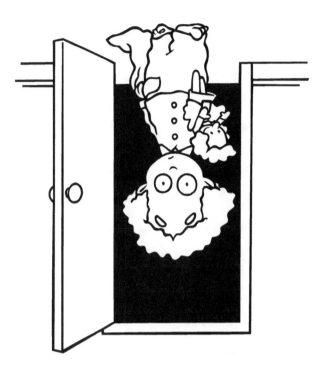

Having a Bad Dream

Draw and/or write what happens next.

1. How does Evie feel?

2. What will Evie probably say to her parents?

3. What might they say to Evie?

4. What could Evie's parents do next?

5. What might Evie do next?

Daniel's grandmother comes over to Daniel's house to visit. She asks Daniel to help her go up the stairs so she can sit on the front porch.

Draw and/or write what happens next.

Grandmother Asks for Help

1. What should Daniel say to his grandmother?

2. What should he do next?

3. Why should Daniel help his grandmother?

4. How will Daniel's grandmother feel when he helps her?

5. What might his grandmother say to Daniel after he helps her?

#BK-293 204 Fold & Say® Social Stories • ©2002 Super Duper® Publications
www.superduperinc.com • 1-800-277-8737

Keith's mom and dad are going out to dinner. Keith's regular babysitter isn't coming over. Keith's mom says, "Keith this is Julie. She'll be babysitting you tonight."

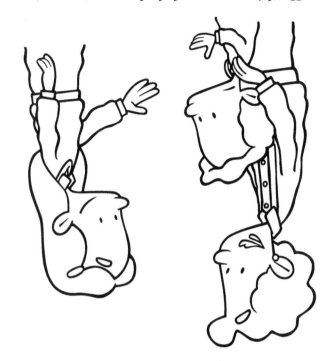

Meeting the New Babysitter

Draw and/or write what happens next.

1. What will Julie probably say next to Keith?

2. What should Keith say back to Julie?

3. What will Keith's parents do next?

4. Why does Keith need a babysitter?

5. What will Julie and Keith do while his parents are out at dinner?

Carl is at his birthday party. He opens a present, but he already has this same toy at home.

Getting the Same Gift Twice

1. How does Carl feel about getting a present he already has?

2. What should Carl NOT say?

3. Why shouldn't Carl say that?

4. How would the person who gave Carl the toy feel if Carl acted disappointed?

5. What should Carl say after opening the present?

Draw and/or write what happens next.

Ernie's friend Kurt is playing inside at Ernie's house. Ernie's mom is outside watering her flowers. Kurt walks up the stairs and slides down the banister in Ernie's house.

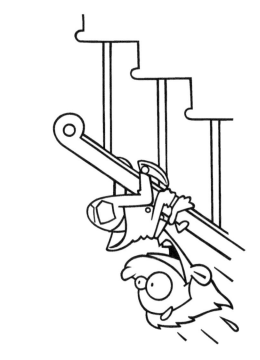

Sliding Down the Banister

Draw and/or write what happens next.

1. What should Ernie say to Kurt?

2. What should Kurt say to Ernie?

3. What would Ernie's mom say if she saw Kurt sliding down the banister?

4. Why doesn't Ernie's mom know what Kurt is doing?

5. What should Ernie do if Kurt keeps sliding down the banister?

Patty hasn't finished her homework yet. Robert rings the doorbell and asks Patty if she can come out to play. Patty remembers that her mom said to finish her homework.

Finishing Work First

Draw and/or write what happens next.

1. What should Patty do?

2. What should Patty say to Robert?

3. What will Patty's mom probably say if Patty does her homework before she plays?

4. What will Patty's mom say if she plays instead of finishing her homework?

5. How will Patty feel if she goes to play instead of finishing her homework?

Meredith asks Theresa if she wants to go over to her house and play in the sprinkler.

Draw and/or write what happens next.

Being Invited Over

1. What should Theresa say to Meredith?

2. What should Theresa do next?

3. Who should Theresa ask to get permission to go to Meredith's?

4. What might happen next?

5. Why does Meredith want to play with Theresa?

Dante's mom is busy cooking dinner. Dante and his little brother want to go to the movies. Dante pulls on her arm, and asks, "Mom, can we go to the movies now?"

Mom Is Busy

Draw and/or write what happens next.

1. What is Dante doing that he shouldn't be doing?

2. Why shouldn't Dante pull on his mom's arm right now?

3. When might be a better time for Dante to talk to his mom?

4. Why should Dante wait until then?

5. What might Dante's mom say to Dante when she is busy?

Alanna and her family are eating breakfast. Alanna and her little brother both reach for the last biscuit at the same time.

Both Wanting the Same Thing

Draw and/or write what happens next.

1. What is the problem?

2. What might happen next?

3. What might Alanna say?

4. What might her little brother say?

5. What should Alanna and her little brother do since they both want the biscuit?

It is Julian's birthday party. Julian's little brother is crying because only Julian got presents.

Draw and/or write what happens next.

Someone Else's Party

1. Why is Julian's little brother crying?

2. Should Julian's little brother be crying?

3. Why didn't Julian's little brother get any presents?

4. What could Julian tell his little brother to make him feel better?

5. What does Julian's little brother need to learn about other people's parties?

Darren's family is going to the mall. Darren and his little brother both want to sit between their parents in the front seat of the car.

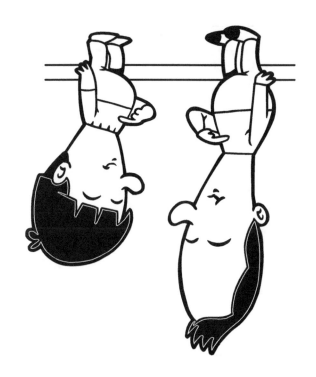

Draw and/or write what happens next.

Sitting in the Front

1. What might Darren and his little brother ask their parents?

2. What should Darren's parents do?

3. Where should Darren and his little brother sit? Why?

4. How will this make the boys feel?

5. What might Darren's parents say to the boys?

Alice is playing with her basketball. Alice's little brother is crying because he wants Alice's ball.

Draw and/or write what happens next.

Someone Wants Your Toy

1. What might Alice say to her little brother?

2. How would this make him feel?

3. What are a few things Alice could do to make her brother stop crying?

4. How could Alice and her little brother share the ball?

5. Why shouldn't Alice just give the ball to her little brother?

Jerry is playing in his room when his little brother walks in. Jerry tells his brother to leave the room. His brother starts crying.

Privacy

Draw and/or write what happens next.

1. Why is Jerry's little brother crying?

2. What did Jerry want his little brother to do?

3. What else could Jerry have said to his brother?

4. What should Jerry do next?

5. Who could help Jerry and his brother solve this problem?

Darlene's parents take Darlene and her little brother to a party. Darlene is chasing her little brother around the table. He is yelling and laughing. Darlene's mom and dad walk over to them.

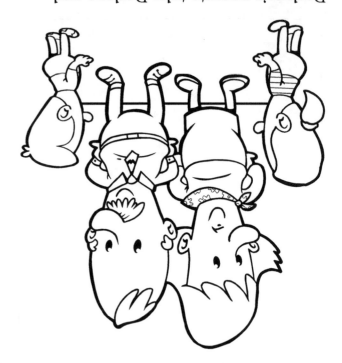

Draw and/or write what happens next.

Using Party Manners

1. What will Darlene's parents probably say to Darlene and her brother?

2. How are they probably feeling towards the children?

3. What should Darlene say to her parents?

4. What should she do next?

5. What should Darlene and her little brother say to the people having the party?

Parker is in her room. It is raining very hard outside. Suddenly, the lights go out.

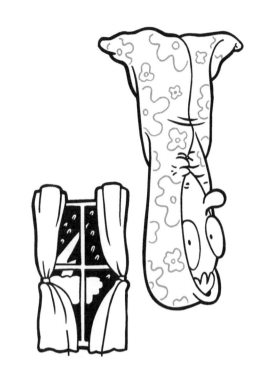

Draw and/or write what happens next.

Getting Scared

1. How will Parker probably feel?

2. What should Parker do?

3. What should Parker NOT do?

4. What will Parker say to her parents?

5. What will Parker's parents probably tell her?

Millie is eating lunch. She wants more spaghetti, but she can't reach it. It is on the other end of the table.

Draw and/or write what happens next.

I Can't Reach It

1. How can Millie get more spaghetti?

2. What can Millie say to get more spaghetti?

3. What will someone in Millie's family do after she asks for more spaghetti?

4. What should Millie say after someone passes her the spaghetti?

5. What will that person say back to Millie?

#BK-293 204 Fold & Say® Social Stories • ©2002 Super Duper® Publications
www.superduperinc.com • 1-800-277-8737

Evan is trying to walk through a crowd of people. Someone is in his way.

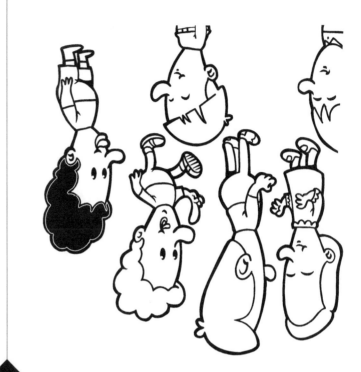

Excuse Me

Draw and/or write what happens next.

1. What is Evan's problem?

2. What could Evan say to the person?

3. What will the person probably say to Evan?

4. What will the person do?

5. What should Evan do if the person will not move out of the way?

Caroline is in the bathroom. She goes to brush her teeth. She squeezes the toothpaste, but nothing comes out.

Draw and/or write what happens next.

I Need to Tell Someone

1. Why is nothing coming out of the toothpaste tube?

2. What should Caroline do next?

3. What will Caroline say to her mom or dad?

4. What will they say to Caroline?

5. What will they do next?

It is snowing outside. Jordan is trying to zip his coat, but he can't.

Needing Help to Zip

Draw and/or write what happens next.

1. How does it feel outside?

2. What should Jordan do if he can't zip his coat?

3. How should he ask someone to help?

4. What will the helper probably do?

5. What should Jordan say to the person who helps him?

Sarah answers the telephone. The man on the line asks if Sheila is home. There is no one in Sarah's house named Sheila.

Sorry, Wrong Number

Draw and/or write what happens next.

1. What should Sarah say to the man?

2. What should she NOT say to the man?

3. Why did the man call Sarah's house?

4. What will the man probably say to Sarah?

5. Should Sarah tell anyone about this phone call? Why?

Emmanuel's mom has to go take a shower. She asks, "Emmanuel, will you please answer the phone while I take a shower? Come get me if Mrs. Jameson calls, okay?"

Answering the Phone for Someone

Draw and/or write what happens next.

1. What should Emmanuel say next?

2. What will his mom probably say?

3. What will Emmanuel's mom go do next?

4. If the phone rings, what should Emmanuel ask the person calling?

5. If Mrs. Jameson calls, what should he say to her before he goes to get his mother?

Jared's mom is on the phone. Jared keeps trying to ask her something.

Interrupting

Draw and/or write what happens next.

1. What is Jared doing that he should not be doing?

2. How does Jared's mom feel?

3. What should Jared do instead of trying to get his mom's attention?

4. Why should Jared wait?

5. What will Jared's mom tell Jared?

Adrian answers the phone. Adrian tells the person on the phone that his mom can't come to the phone. The lady says, "Tell your mom to meet June at 6:30 instead of 6:00, okay?"

Draw and/or write what happens next.

Taking a Message for Someone

1. What should Adrian say to the lady?

2. How can Adrian remember the message?

3. What should Adrian do with the message?

4. Why is it important for Adrian to give his mom the message?

5. What will Adrian's mom probably say to him when he gives her the message?

Jean is shopping with her aunt in the toy store. She keeps wandering away from her aunt. Jean's aunt keeps telling her to stay close by her.

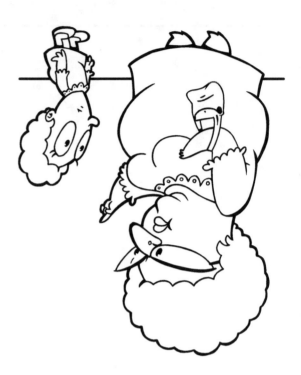

Staying With a Grown-Up

Draw and/or write what happens next.

1. Why is Jean's aunt telling her to stay close to her?

2. What could happen if Jean wanders off?

3. How will Jean's aunt feel if Jean gets lost?

4. What can Jean do to let her aunt know she is listening?

5. What might Jean say to her aunt about her wandering off?

Justin goes to the bank with his mom. The lady behind the counter asks Justin if he wants a lollipop.

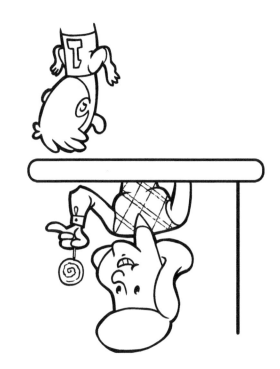

Draw and/or write what happens next.

Getting a Treat

1. What should Justin say if he wants the lollipop?

2. What should Justin say if he doesn't want it?

3. What should Justin say to the lady if he takes the lollipop?

4. How will this make the lady behind the counter feel?

5. What will Justin's mom say to Justin if he uses good manners?

©2002 Super Duper Publications

Raymond's mom sees one of her friends at the store. His mom's friend says, "Hi, what's your name?" to Raymond.

Draw and/or write what happens next.

Meeting Mom's Friend

1. What should Raymond say?

2. What should you do when you meet someone for the first time?

3. What might Mom's friend say next to Raymond?

4. How could Raymond find out the name of his mom's friend?

5. What will Raymond's mom say about Raymond's good manners?

Louis is in the shoe store. The saleslady is very nice. She helps Louis pick out a new pair of shoes, but Louis does not like the pair she shows him.

Draw and/or write what happens next.

Not Liking Something

1. What could Louis say to the lady?

2. How should he say it?

3. How might the lady feel?

4. What will she probably say to Louis?

5. What will she probably do next?

Violet is in the toy aisle at the store. She looks around, but she can't find her mom.

Draw and/or write what happens next.

Getting Lost

1. What should Violet do next?

2. Who should she look for if she can't find her mom?

3. What should she say to that person?

4. What will the helper do?

5. What will Violet's mom say when she finds her?

Becky is at the grocery store with her family. She accidentally knocks over a bottle of ketchup and it spills on the floor.

Making a Mess

Draw and/or write what happens next.

1. How does Becky feel?

2. What should Becky do now?

3. What should Becky say to one of the workers in the store?

4. What will the store person say to Becky?

5. What might Becky say to the worker after the spill is cleaned up?

Nigel's mom has to buy a new dress. Nigel doesn't want to be in the dress store with his mom.

Draw and/or write what happens next.

Going Shopping with Mom

1. Should Nigel tell his mom he wants to leave? Why or why not?

2. How should Nigel act while his mom shops?

3. What could Nigel do while his mom shops?

4. What will Nigel's mom probably say if Nigel starts to complain about being at the dress store?

5. What will Nigel's mom say if he sits and waits quietly while she shops?

Cora saved up her allowance to buy a new toy. The lady in the store tells Cora that they are all out of the toy she wanted, but she could check back again in a week.

Not Getting What You Wanted to Buy

Draw and/or write what happens next.

1. How does Cora probably feel?

2. What should Cora say to the lady?

3. What should Cora do now?

4. How will Cora feel if the toy is out of stock again next week?

5. How will Cora feel if the store has the toy next week?

Trent is in the store with his dad. Trent sees his friend Jade in the store with her dad. Jade smiles at Trent and waves.

Draw and/or write what happens next.

Introducing People

1. Why is Jade smiling at Trent?

2. What should Trent do next?

3. What might Jade say to Trent and his dad?

4. What should Trent say to Jade and her dad?

5. What will Trent's dad say to Jade's dad?

Marcel is in the grocery store with his mom. He sees some people who are communicating with their hands. He stares at them and points.

Not Staring

Draw and/or write what happens next.

1. What is Marcel doing that he shouldn't be doing?

2. How will the people feel if Marcel stares and points?

3. What could Marcel ask his mom?

4. Why are the people talking like that?

5. What will Marcel's mom tell him?

Patrick is walking with his mom in the grocery store. He looks down and sees a wallet on the floor.

It's Not Mine

Draw and/or write what happens next.

1. What might Patrick do next?

2. What should Patrick do if he picks up the wallet?

3. Where could Patrick bring the wallet?

4. What might happen to the wallet after that?

5. What could the person who owns the wallet say if he gets it back?

Tyler and his family are in a restaurant. Tyler picks up his food with his fingers. Tyler's dad looks at Tyler and starts to say something.

Draw and/or write what happens next.

Eating Politely in a Restaurant

1. What will Tyler's dad probably say to Tyler?

2. Why doesn't Tyler's dad want Tyler to eat with his fingers?

3. How will Tyler's dad feel if Tyler eats with his fingers?

4. What should Tyler say to his dad?

5. Is it okay to eat some types of food with your fingers? What types?

Chloe is at a cafeteria with her family. The lady asks Chloe if she wants gravy on her mashed potatoes. Chloe doesn't want gravy.

Draw and/or write what happens next.

Saying "No, Thank You"

1. What does the lady want to know?

2. What should Chloe say to the lady?

3. How should she say it?

4. What will the lady say to Chloe then?

5. How would Chloe feel if the lady put gravy on her potatoes?

Mandy is in a restaurant with her family. Mandy does not have a fork or spoon. Everyone else has silverware.

What About Me?

Draw and/or write what happens next.

1. Who should Mandy talk to?

2. What should she ask this person?

3. What will this person say to Mandy?

4. What will this person do?

5. What should Mandy do if she drops her fork on the floor by mistake?

Wanting Something Different

Marty is in a restaurant with his friends. His hamburger has cheese melted on it. Marty didn't want cheese.

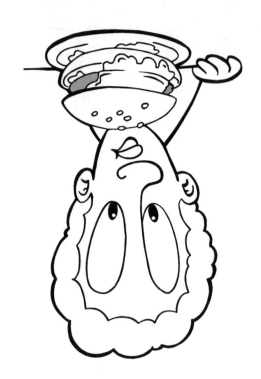

Draw and/or write what happens next.

1. Who should Marty talk to?

2. What should he say to this person?

3. What will this person say to Marty?

4. What will happen next?

5. How would Marty feel if he didn't say anything about the cheese?

Sadie's team was playing soccer. Sadie scored two goals and the team won. The coach walks up to Sadie after the game.

Feeling Good

Draw and/or write what happens next.

1. What will the coach say to Sadie?

2. Why will he say that?

3. What will Sadie say to her coach?

4. How will Sadie feel?

5. What does Sadie's coach think about Sadie right now?

Miss Duncan sneezes. Henry is looking at her.

Sneezing

Draw and/or write what happens next.

1. What might Henry say next?

2. Why should Henry say something?

3. What will Miss Duncan say to Henry?

4. What should Henry say if Miss Duncan sneezes again?

5. What should you do when you sneeze?

Angela is playing in the yard. Miss Sharon her neighbor, walks over from her house and asks Angela if her mom is home.

Answering Someone

1. What should Angela say?

2. Why should Angela talk to Miss Sharon?

3. Why is Miss Sharon asking Angela this question?

4. What might Angela ask Miss Sharon?

5. What should Angela do next?

Draw and/or write what happens next.

Mr. Paul sees Juan after his family returns from summer vacation. He says, "Hi Juan, tell me about your vacation."

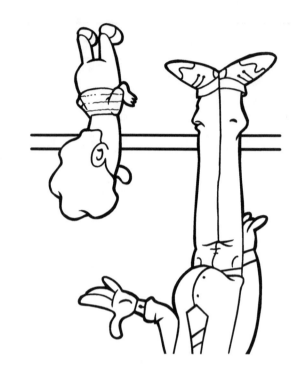

Draw and/or write what happens next.

Telling About Your Vacation

1. What kinds of things could Juan tell Mr. Paul?

2. What questions might Mr. Paul ask Juan about his vacation?

3. Why is Mr. Paul asking Juan about his vacation?

4. How does Juan feel about Mr. Paul asking about his vacation?

5. What else could Juan do to show Mr. Paul what his vacation was like?

#BK-293 204 Fold & Say® Social Stories • ©2002 Super Duper® Publications
www.superduperinc.com • 1-800-277-8737

Mr. Robertson walks up to Steven. He sticks his hand out and says, "Hello, my name is Mr. Robertson."

Shaking Hands

1. Why does Mr. Robertson have his hand out?

2. What should Steven do next?

3. What should Steven say to Mr. Robertson?

4. Why is Mr. Robertson telling Steven his name?

5. Should Steven tell Mr. Robertson his name? Why or why not?

Draw and/or write what happens next.

David's Aunt Jaymie comes over to visit. She says, "David, I have a new train set for you."

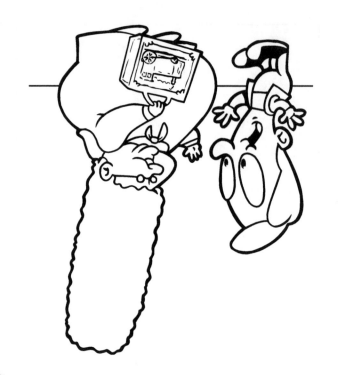

Draw and/or write what happens next.

Getting a Gift

1. What should David say next?

2. What will his Aunt Jaymie say?

3. How does David feel?

4. Why did she give David a new toy?

5. What should David do after Aunt Jaymie leaves to go home?

Malcolm is walking through the doorway. A lady is behind him with a baby in a stroller.

Going In

Draw and/or write what happens next.

1. What should Malcolm do?

2. What should Malcolm NOT do?

3. What will the lady say if Malcolm holds the door for her?

4. What will Malcolm say to the lady?

5. How will the lady feel?

When Someone Does a Mean Thing

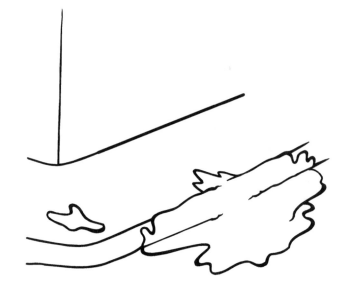

Lawrence is walking with his little brother down the street. A big kid on a bicycle splashes mud on them with his bike. Lawrence's little brother starts to cry.

Draw and/or write what happens next.

1. How do Lawrence and his little brother feel?

2. What might Lawrence say to the big kid?

3. What should the big kid say after Lawrence talks to him?

4. What could Lawrence tell his little brother?

5. What might Lawrence do for his little brother?

Dean is at karate class. It is just finishing. Dean thinks that he doesn't want to go to karate anymore. Dean walks over to his mom.

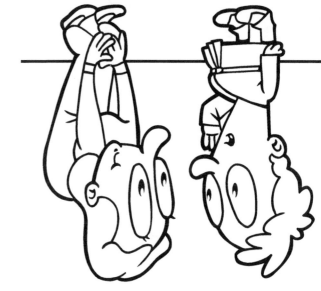

Not Wanting to Go Anymore

Draw and/or write what happens next.

1. What could Dean say to his mom?

2. How should he say it?

3. What might his mom say to Dean?

4. Why doesn't Dean want to go to karate anymore?

5. What might Dean's mom tell him to do?

Karla and her family are in line waiting to pose for a family picture. The line to take pictures is long. Karla keeps asking when it will be their turn.

Waiting Patiently

1. How does Karla feel?

2. What will Karla's mom and dad probably say to Karla?

3. What could Karla do while she is waiting?

4. What will Karla's parent's say to her if they see her waiting quietly and patiently?

5. How will Karla feel when it is finally their turn?

Draw and/or write what happens next.

#BK-293 204 Fold & Say® Social Stories • ©2002 Super Duper® Publications
www.superduperinc.com • 1-800-277-8737

Ben and his family are at "family night" at the bookstore. The lady is reading a story to the children. Ben says loudly, "This is boring. This is for babies." Everyone looks at Ben. His mom and dad frown.

Draw and/or write what happens next.

Not Wanting to Do What Everyone Else Wants to Do

1. Why are Ben's parents frowning?

2. What did Ben say that he shouldn't have said?

3. Why did Ben say what he said?

4. What should Ben have done instead?

5. What might Ben's parents say to him?

Tom's family goes to the airport to pick up his Aunt Rita, who is walking down the terminal. They are all smiling at each other.

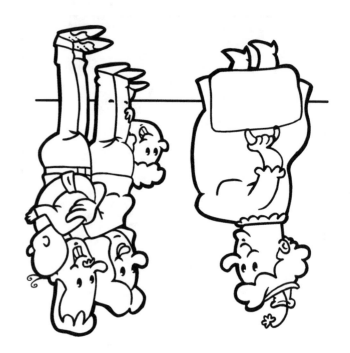

Draw and/or write what happens next.

Picking Up a Relative

1. Why is everyone smiling?

2. How did Aunt Rita get to the airport?

3. What will Tom's family probably say to Aunt Rita?

4. What might Aunt Rita say to them?

5. Where will they all go now?

Kyle is walking with his mom. They come to a busy street that they have to cross. Kyle steps out into the street. Kyle's mom grabs his arm.

Watching for Cars

Draw and/or write what happens next.

1. Why did Kyle's mom grab his arm?

2. What could happen if Kyle walked into the street?

3. What will Kyle's mom probably tell Kyle now?

4. What should Kyle do?

5. Why do we need to look both ways before crossing the street?

Sharon and her mom go to their friend's house to see the new baby. They have a gift. Marcia answers the door.

Seeing Someone's New Baby

Draw and/or write what happens next.

1. What will Marcia probably say?

2. What might Sharon's mom say to Marcia?

3. What will Sharon's mom do with the baby gift?

4. Why did Sharon and her mom bring a gift?

5. How will Marcia feel about the gift?

Ashley is holding Mrs. Johnson's baby. The baby starts to cry.

Holding a Baby

Draw and/or write what happens next.

1. How does Ashley feel about the baby crying?

2. What will Ashley probably do?

3. What might Ashley tell Mrs. Johnson?

4. What could Mrs. Johnson say to Ashley?

5. What might Ashley do with the baby if it keeps crying?

Sam is at a barbecue with his family. He sees that Mrs. Garcia looks very tired. Mrs. Garcia is standing up with her new baby because there are no more chairs for her to sit on.

Draw and/or write what happens next.

Giving Up Your Seat

1. How could Sam get Mrs. Garcia a seat?

2. What words should he say to Mrs. Garcia?

3. What will Mrs. Garcia probably say to Sam?

4. How will Mrs. Garcia probably feel after Sam talks with her?

5. How will Sam probably feel?

#BK-293 204 Fold & Say® Social Stories • ©2002 Super Duper® Publications
www.superduperinc.com • 1-800-277-8737

Sarah's grandmother had surgery. She is in the hospital. Sarah walks into her hospital room.

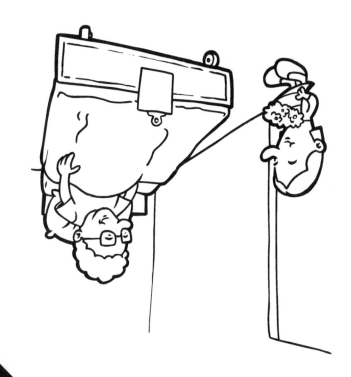

Draw and/or write what happens next.

Visiting at the Hospital

1. What might Sarah say to her grandmother?

2. What will Sarah's grandmother say to her?

3. How will Sarah's grandmother feel about Sarah's visit?

4. What could Sarah bring to her grandmother to make her feel better?

5. What may Sarah's grandmother say to Sarah when she sees what Sarah brought her?

Raymond is swimming in the pool at the park. Raymond's mom says, "Raymond, time to get out. It's time to go home." Raymond doesn't want to go home yet.

Draw and/or write what happens next.

It's Time to Go

1. What might Raymond say to his mom?

2. What should Raymond do?

3. What should Raymond NOT say and do?

4. How will Raymond's mom feel if Raymond gets out of the pool?

5. How will Raymond's mom feel if he stays in the pool?

©2002 Super Duper® Publications

Jasmine is at a parade with her family. Jasmine catches a stuffed animal. The little boy standing next to Jasmine is crying because he wanted to catch it.

Giving to Someone Younger Than You

©2002 Super Duper® Publications

Draw and/or write what happens next.

1. How does Jasmine feel about catching the stuffed animal?

2. What would be a nice thing for Jasmine to do?

3. Why should Jasmine be nice to the little boy?

4. What will Jasmine's parents think if Jasmine does a nice thing for the boy?

5. What will the little boy's mom say to Jasmine if she is nice to her son?

Lawrence and his family are at a football game. Lawrence and his brother go up to the person dressed up as the team's mascot, a tiger. Lawrence's little brother starts screaming.

Someone Is Scared

Draw and/or write what happens next.

1. Why is Lawrence's little brother screaming?

2. Why isn't Lawrence screaming?

3. What should Lawrence tell his little brother to make him feel better?

4. What should the person dressed up as the tiger say?

5. What could the person dressed up as the tiger do to help Lawrence?

#BK-293 204 Fold & Say® Social Stories • ©2002 Super Duper® Publications
www.superduperinc.com • 1-800-277-8737

Asking Permission

Abby is walking with her dad. They see a man walking a dog. Abby wants to pet the dog.

Draw and/or write what happens next.

1. What should Abby do if she wants to pet the dog?

2. Why should Abby ask the dog's owner if she can pet the dog first?

3. How might Abby ask this question?

4. What might the man say to Abby?

5. What will Abby say if the man lets her pet the dog?

Paul and his mom are riding bikes together. Paul does not stop for the stop sign.

Draw and/or write what happens next.

Being Careful

1. What should Paul have done?

2. What will Paul's mom say to him?

3. Why did Paul's mom want him to stop?

4. What could happen to Paul?

5. What are some other rules to follow when riding a bike, a scooter or roller skating?

Dean is talking to his grandmother about karate class. Dean just moved up to the next belt level in karate.

Being Proud

Draw and/or write what happens next.

1. What might Dean tell his grandmother?

2. Why is he telling her this?

3. What will she say back to Dean?

4. How does Dean feel about moving up in his class?

5. What does Dean's grandmother think of Dean's new belt?

Cooperating

Brenda goes to the dentist. Brenda sits very still. The dentist tells Brenda to open her mouth wide.

Draw and/or write what happens next.

1. What should Brenda do next?

2. What will the dentist do to Brenda?

3. How will that make Brenda feel?

4. What will Brenda's mom say about the way Brenda acted?

5. What will the dentist probably say to Brenda's mom?

Harry is at the doctor's office. He got a shot today. The nurse says, "I am very proud of you for being so good. Do you want a sticker?"

Draw and/or write what happens next.

Being Good at the Doctor's

1. What might Harry say to the nurse?

2. What will the nurse do if Harry says he wants a sticker?

3. Why did the nurse offer Harry a sticker?

4. What will Harry's parents think about the way Harry acted?

5. What will Harry's parents say to Harry about the way he acted?

Jack's mom takes him to the doctor for his check-up. Jack is crying and screaming in the waiting room.

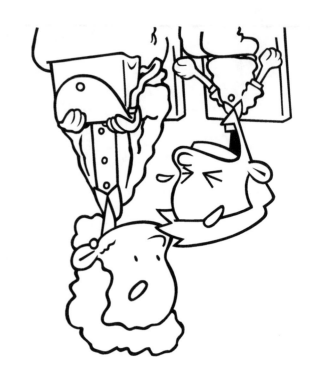

Draw and/or write what happens next.

Being Afraid of the Doctor

1. Why is Jack crying?

2. Why should Jack stop crying?

3. What might Jack's mom say to Jack to comfort him?

4. What might help Jack calm down?

5. What do the other people in the waiting room think about Jack?

Lacey is at her friend Dane's house. Dane offers Lacey a cookie. Lacey grabs a handful of cookies.

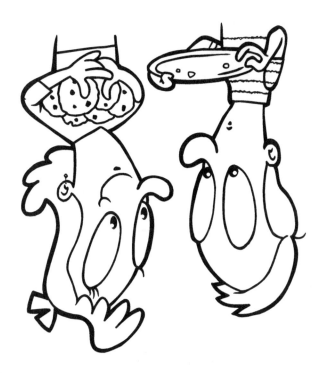

Taking Too Much

Draw and/or write what happens next.

1. What is Lacey doing that is "bad manners"?

2. Why is it rude or not good manners to grab a bunch of cookies?

3. What should Lacey do instead?

4. What might Dane say to Lacey?

5. What should Dane do if Lacey tries to grab more cookies?

Kyle and his friend are at the zoo. Kyle's friend wants to see the monkeys, but Kyle wants to see the tigers first.

Draw and/or write what happens next.

Deciding Where to Go

1. How can the two boys decide where to go first?

2. What should they say to each other?

3. How should they say it?

4. Why shouldn't they argue or use mean words to decide about where to go?

5. How will they feel if they work things out?

Wanting to Do Something Different

Alice and her family are having fun at the amusement park. Alice's little brother wants to go on the merry-go-round, but Alice wants to go on the Ferris wheel. Alice's little brother starts to cry.

Draw and/or write what happens next.

1. Why is Alice's little brother crying?

2. What might Alice tell her little brother?

3. How could they go on both rides?

4. What might Alice's parents say to them?

5. How will Alice's parents feel if Alice helps her brother stop crying?

Seeing Someone You Know At a New Place

Jessie's dad walks him into the play area on his first day at summer camp. Jessie is feeling afraid. Suddenly, a new boy from Jessie's neighborhood runs up to Jessie. He says, "Hey Jessie! Are you coming, too?"

Draw and/or write what happens next.

1. Why did the boy run up to Jessie?

2. What might Jessie say to the boy?

3. How does Jessie feel about seeing the boy?

4. Does Jessie feel afraid about camp anymore?

5. What might the two boys do next?

Jeff is playing at Taylor's house. Taylor points to a new train set. Taylor says, "Hey Jeff, look what I got for my birthday!"

Seeing Someone's New Present

Draw and/or write what happens next.

1. What should Jeff do next?

2. What might Jeff say to Taylor?

3. Why should Jeff look at Taylor's train set?

4. How will that make Taylor feel?

5. How will Jeff feel if Taylor invites him to play with his new train set?

Not Having Enough Information

Stephanie says, "Maggie went with me yesterday." Marcos doesn't know who Maggie is or where they went.

Draw and/or write what happens next.

1. What should Marcos ask Stephanie?

2. What additional information might Stephanie tell Marcos?

3. Why does Marcos need to know more information?

4. What else could Stephanie say or do to help Marcos understand?

5. What can Marcos do or say to let Stephanie know he understands?

Devin and Meredith are at Mitchell's house. They come inside after swimming in the pool. Mitchell and Meredith go put their wet towels in the laundry basket. Devin throws his wet towel on the floor.

Putting Things Where They Belong

Draw and/or write what happens next.

1. What should Mitchell and Meredith tell Devin?

2. What should Devin do with his wet towel?

3. Why should Devin pick up his towel?

4. What might Mitchell's mom say to Devin if he leaves his towel on the floor?

5. What might Devin say to Mitchells' mom?

Standing Too Close

McKenna is talking to Steven. McKenna is standing very close to Steven. Steven does not like how close McKenna is standing to him. He wants McKenna to move.

Draw and/or write what happens next.

1. How does Steven feel?

2. What should Steven do?

3. Why does Steven want McKenna to move?

4. Why shouldn't people stand too close to other people?

5. What might McKenna say to Steven if Steven asks her to move?

Mei-Ling likes Will's bouncy ball. Will says, "Here, you can have it," to Mei-Ling.

Saying Thanks

Draw and/or write what happens next.

1. How does that make Mei-Ling feel?

2. What might Mei-Ling say to Will?

3. What could Will say to Mei-Ling if she says, "thank you"?

4. What could Mei-Ling do for Will to show her thanks?

5. How does it make Will feel to give Mei-Ling his ball?

Adrian tells Bobby that she has a new baby sister.

Someone Has a New Baby

Draw and/or write what happens next.

1. What might Bobby ask Adrian?

2. How does Adrian feel about her new sister?

3. Why is she telling Bobby about the baby?

4. What might Bobby want to know about the baby?

5. What can you tell us about your brother or sister?

Tom, Peter and Oscar are running to see who can reach the tree first. Oscar is the fastest runner.

Draw and/or write what happens next.

Not Winning

1. Who will get to the tree first?

2. What will Tom and Peter do once Oscar reaches the tree?

3. How will Tom and Peter feel?

4. How will Oscar feel?

5. What is a nice thing that Oscar could say to Tom and Peter?

Robert is talking with John. Jason walks over to the boys and makes fun of the way Robert talks.

Draw and/or write what happens next.

Hearing Someone Tease

1. How will Robert feel?

2. Why should Jason NOT make fun of Robert?

3. What should John and Robert tell Jason?

4. How will Robert feel about what John says?

5. Why isn't it nice to tease other people?

Ashten is playing in her playpen at the park. Her mom is busy talking. Hannah and John are at the park too. Hannah sees Ashten drop her teddy bear and begin to cry.

Helping Out

Draw and/or write what happens next.

1. What should Hannah do next?

2. Why should Hannah do something to help Ashten?

3. How will Hannah feel if she helps Ashten?

4. What will Ashten's mom say to Hannah?

5. How will Ashten feel if Hannah helps her?

It is January. Elliott asks Rivkah what he got for Christmas. Rivkah says that his family celebrates Hanukkah instead of Christmas.

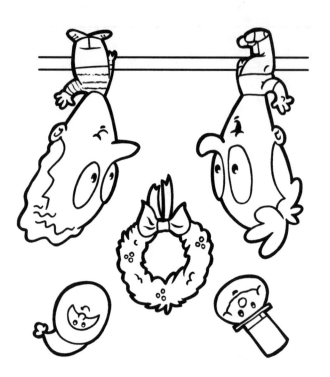

Draw and/or write what happens next.

Doing Something Different

1. What should Elliott say next to Rivkah?

2. What should Elliott NOT say?

3. What might Rivkah ask Elliott?

4. Why do some families do different things on holidays?

5. What are some things your family does on a holiday?

Andrew has a new magazine. Tom wants to see it.

Asking to Share

Draw and/or write what happens next.

1. What should Tom say if he wants to see the magazine?

2. What should Andrew say to Tom?

3. What should Tom say when he is finished looking at the magazine?

4. What will Tom think of Andrew if he shares?

5. How do people feel when we share things with them?

Peter and Kendall are playing basketball. Kendall tells Peter that he can't shoot the ball very well.

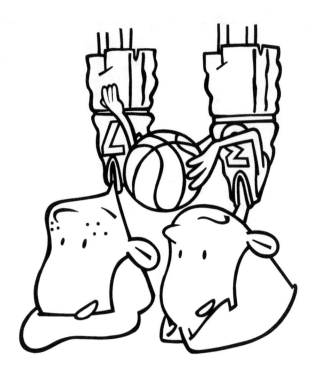

Not Being Nice

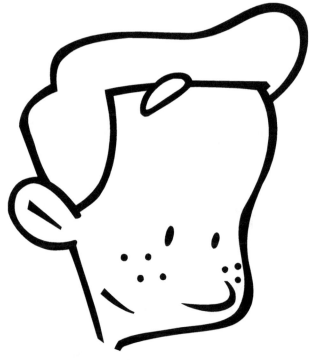

Draw and/or write what happens next.

1. Did Kendall speak nicely to Peter?

2. Why shouldn't people say mean things to each other?

3. How does Peter feel about Kendall's words?

4. What might Peter say to Kendall?

5. What could Kendall do instead of telling Peter he can't shoot?

Tara and her friends are swimming. Tara is splashing in the water. Rachel asks Tara to stop splashing her.

Being Nice In the Water

1. What should Tara say to Rachel?

2. What should Tara do?

3. Why should Tara do that?

4. How would Rachel feel if Tara splashes her again?

5. What might Rachel say if Tara stops splashing her?

Draw and/or write what happens next.

Isabelle's cat ran away. Crystal walks up to Isabelle.

I'm Sorry You're Sad

Draw and/or write what happens next.

1. How does Isabelle feel?

2. What might Crystal say to Isabelle?

3. What will Isabelle probably tell Crystal?

4. What might Crystal do?

5. What could they do together to make Isabelle feel better?

Ryan tells Chuck that his family is going on vacation.

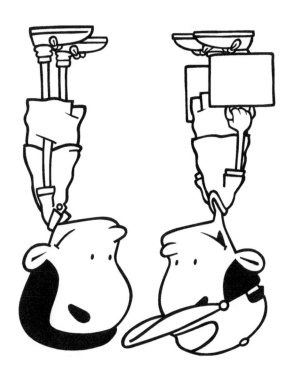

Draw and/or write what happens next.

Asking For More Information

1. What might Chuck ask next?

2. What might Ryan tell Chuck?

3. How does Ryan feel about his vacation?

4. Why would Chuck ask about Ryan's vacation?

5. What could Ryan ask Chuck?

Daniel got dressed for his baseball game. It is the last game of the tournament. Daniel is very excited. His mom says the weather person predicted it would rain today.

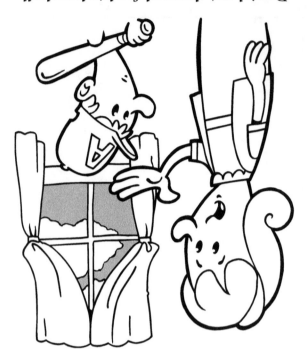

Draw and/or write what happens next.

Feeling Disappointed

1. How does Daniel feel?

2. What should Daniel say to his mom?

3. What should Daniel NOT do or say?

4. What does "disappointed" mean?

5. What could Daniel do if the game is postponed?

Mikayla is one of Robert's best friends. Mikayla's dad told her they will be moving in two weeks. Mikayla walks up to Robert.

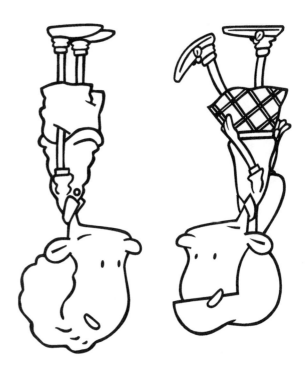

When Someone is Moving

Draw and/or write what happens next.

1. How does Mikayla feel?

2. What will Mikayla tell Robert?

3. What might Robert say?

4. How will Robert and Mikayla feel?

5. How can Robert and Mikayla stay friends and communicate after she moves?

Toby and his friends tried out for the soccer team. They are reading the list of names of the boys who made the team. Toby's name is not on the list.

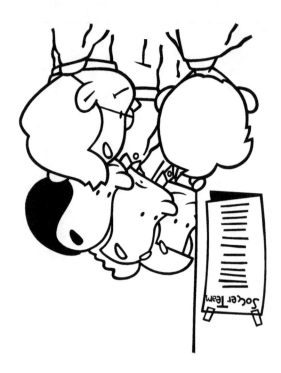

Draw and/or write what happens next.

Not Making the Team

1. Why is Toby's name not on the list?

2. How does Toby feel?

3. What should Toby's friends say to him?

4. What should they NOT say?

5. What could Toby say to them to show he is happy that his friends made the team?

#BK-293 204 Fold & Say® Social Stories • ©2002 Super Duper® Publications
www.superduperinc.com • 1-800-277-8737

Getting a Ride Home

Heather was at soccer. Her mom told her to ask Mrs. Jenny for a ride home. Mrs. Jenny is now at Heather's house. Heather is getting out of Mrs. Jenny's van.

Draw and/or write what happens next.

1. What should Heather say to Mrs. Jenny?

2. What will Mrs. Jenny probably say?

3. What will Heather's mom say to Mrs. Jenny when she sees her again?

4. Why will Heather's mom say that to Mrs. Jenny?

5. Will Mrs. Jenny give Heather a ride home again?

Juan drank all of his juice. He wants more.

Draw and/or write what happens next.

Wanting More

1. Who does Juan need to talk to?

2. What should he say?

3. What might that person tell him?

4. What could that person do?

5. What should Juan say if he gets more juice?

When a Friend Isn't There

Paul goes to summer camp. He looks for his friend Jeremy, that he plays with every day, but Jeremy isn't there.

Draw and/or write what happens next.

1. How does Paul feel when he doesn't see Jeremy?

2. What could be a reason why Jeremy isn't at camp?

3. What should Paul do now?

4. Could Paul play with someone else?

5. How might Paul ask someone to play with him?

Shane is playing in his neighborhood. Some big kids are playing with a ball. Shane asks if he can play too. One of the big kids says that Shane can't play because he's not as old as they are.

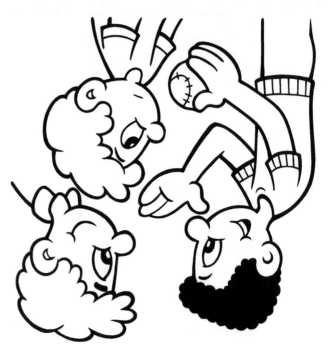

Being Left Out

Draw and/or write what happens next.

1. How does Shane feel?

2. How did the older boy treat Shane?

3. What could Shane say now?

4. What might Shane do now?

5. What could one of the other big kids in the group say that would make Shane feel better?

Someone Wants to Take Something

Trent and Michael are playing at Trent's house. It is time for Michael to go home. Michael picks up Trent's favorite toy car and asks if he can have it.

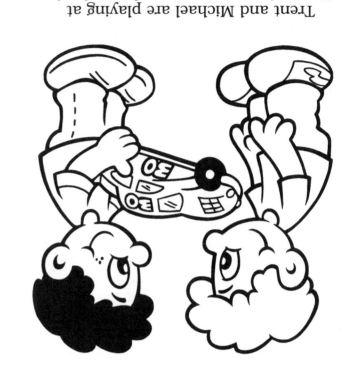

Draw and/or write what happens next.

1. What might Trent tell Michael if Trent doesn't want to give him the car?

2. What might Michael say to Trent?

3. What might Michael do?

4. Why shouldn't Michael expect to take home Trent's toy car?

5. What should Trent do if Michael takes his toy car home without Trent's permission?

Albert is sleeping over at Brad's house. It is dark in Brad's room. Albert usually sleeps with a night light on. Albert is afraid of the dark.

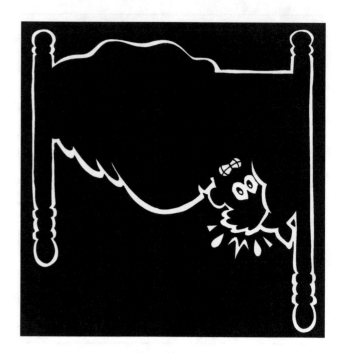

Being Afraid

1. What might Albert say to Brad?

2. Should Brad laugh at Albert? Why or why not?

3. What could Brad say to help Albert feel better?

4. Who should the boys talk with if Albert remains scared?

5. What could they do about this problem?

Draw and/or write what happens next.

Needing to Stop

Danny is going to the beach for the day with his friend. They have been riding in the car for a little while. Danny needs to go to the bathroom.

Draw and/or write what happens next.

1. Who should Danny talk to?

2. What should Danny say to this person?

3. How should Danny ask?

4. What will this person probably say?

5. What should Danny say to that person after they stop to let him use the bathroom?

Austin goes to Everett's house for the first time. Austin meets Everett's brother, who goes to another school and is in a classroom for kids with special needs.

Draw and/or write what happens next.

Meeting Someone Who Is Special

1. What should Austin say when he is introduced to Everett's brother?

2. What should Austin NOT say to Everett's brother?

3. Why should Austin talk to Everett's brother like he talks to everyone else?

4. What are "special needs"?

5. How would Everett feel if Austin was not nice to his brother?

Marcus goes to a costume party. He sees Jake, who has on the same costume as Marcus.

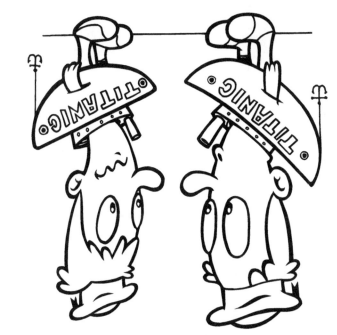

Wearing the Same Costume

Draw and/or write what happens next.

1. How does Marcus feel?

2. How does Jake feel?

3. What might Marcus say to Jake?

4. What might Jake say to Marcus?

5. What should other people at the party say to both boys?

Harold gives Sarah an invitation to his birthday party on Saturday.

Draw and/or write what happens next.

Going to a Party

1. Why did Harold invite Sarah to his party?

2. What should Sarah say to Harold?

3. How does Sarah feel?

4. What does Sarah need to do before she goes to the party?

5. Why will she do that?

Brady and Oscar are playing a game. Oscar loses. Brady laughs at Oscar.

It's Not Funny

Draw and/or write what happens next.

1. Why is Brady laughing?

2. Should Brady laugh at Oscar? Why or why not?

3. How does Oscar feel when Brady laughs at him?

4. What might Oscar say to Brady?

5. What should Oscar do when he wins the game?

Mikayla is at the Duncan's house. She needs to blow her nose. She is looking for a tissue, but doesn't know where to find one.

Needing Something

Draw and/or write what happens next.

1. What should Mikayla do?

2. What should she say to someone in the Duncan family?

3. What will that person tell her?

4. What should Mikayla NOT do?

5. What should Mikayla say after she gets a tissue?

Patty and Maria are talking. Mei-Ling walks up. Maria says, "Happy Birthday," to Mei-Ling. Patty didn't know it was Mei-Ling's birthday.

Saying "Happy Birthday"

Draw and/or write what happens next.

1. What will Mei-Ling say to Maria?

2. What should Patty say to Mei-Ling?

3. What will Mei-Ling say to Patty?

4. Why is it nice manners to wish someone a "Happy Birthday"?

5. What else might the girls talk about?

Weston, Katie, and Christopher are playing a game. All of them want to go first.

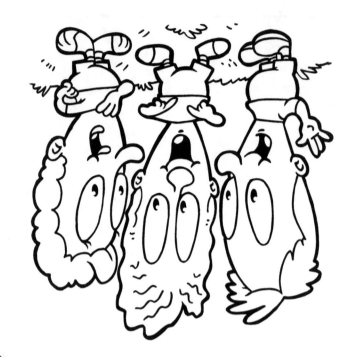

Draw and/or write what happens next.

Going First

1. How many people can go first?

2. How could the kids pick who will go first?

3. What would happen if everyone got angry because they couldn't be first?

4. How will they choose who goes second?

5. Why is it important to work out problems you have?

Choosing Nicely

Kyle, Ashley and Jude are playing a game. They are picking out what color they want to be. Kyle says, "I want to be blue," but Jude grabs the blue piece from Kyle's hand.

Draw and/or write what happens next.

1. What should Kyle do next?

2. What did Jude do that he should NOT have done?

3. How does Kyle feel?

4. What could Jude do to make Kyle feel better?

5. How could the boys decide who will get the blue marker?

Angel walks up to Harry. She says, "Harry, I love your new shoes."

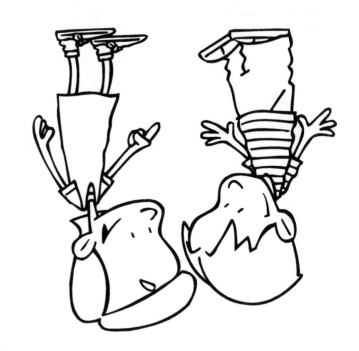

Draw and/or write what happens next.

Getting A Compliment

1. How does Harry feel?

2. What should Harry say to Angel?

3. What is a "compliment"?

4. How do people feel after they receive a compliment?

5. Why do we give compliments to other people?

I practice good social skills!

This Award is Presented to

_____
Student's name

By _____
SLP

On _____
Date

I practice good social skills at home!

This Award is Presented to

_____
Student's name

By _____
SLP

On _____
Date

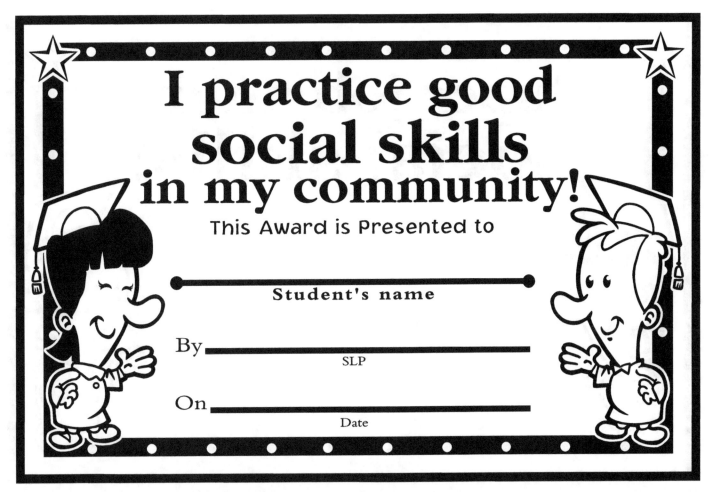

Questions

1._____

2._____

3._____

4._____

5._____

Draw and/or write what happens next.

#BK-293 204 Fold & Say® Social Stories • ©2002 Super Duper® Publications
www.superduperinc.com • 1-800-277-8737

©2002 Super Duper® Publications

Notes

Notes